7-02

DATE DUE		
AUG 07 2007	MAR 09 2008	
FEB 09 2008	OCT 18 2008	
JUN 14 2008	MAR 31 2009	
JUL 13 2009	OCT 22 2009	

Voice
Power

Using Your Voice to

Captivate, Persuade,

and Command Attention

RENEE GRANT-WILLIAMS

AMACOM

AMERICAN MANAGEMENT ASSOCIATION

New York • Atlanta • Brussels • Buenos Aires • Chicago • London • Mexico City
San Francisco • Shanghai • Tokyo • Toronto • Washington, D.C.

7-02

Special discounts on bulk quantities of AMACOM books are available to corporations, professional associations, and other organizations. For details, contact Special Sales Department, AMACOM, a division of American Management Association, 1601 Broadway, New York, NY 10019.
Tel.: 212-903-8316. Fax: 212-903-8083.
Web site: www.amacombooks.org

This publication is designed to provide accurate and authoritative information in regard to the subject matter covered. It is sold with the understanding that the publisher is not engaged in rendering legal, accounting, or other professional service. If legal advice or other expert assistance is required, the services of a competent professional person should be sought.

Library of Congress Cataloging-in-Publications data has been applied for and is on record at the Library of Congress.

Printing number

10   9   8   7   6   5   4   3   2

To Elvis; my Mom; Miss Sue Green; my Father; Andrew Carnegie; and the Ridgeway Free Public Library, my second home as a child

Contents

Acknowledgments

My deepest thanks to Jeff Herman, Ellen Kadin, Elaine Collins, Jonell Polansky, Jody Faison, Sharon Sparks, Susan Rodiek, Penny Rahe, Gene Narmore, Tina Van Horne, Candy Plant, Jeff Slutsky, Alexis Faith, Dr. Barry Yarborough, Catherine Darnell, Diane Waller, Katy Peake, Sandy Smith, David Moser, Denny Pemberton, Jon Rodiek, Doug Fulmer, Danyell Henry, Carol Grace Anderson, Jill Eatherly, Renee Copeland, and Kate Sansing.

That is what learning is. You suddenly understand something you've understood all your life, but in a new way.

—Doris Lessing

voice
production
techniques

Your Voice Speaks Volumes

HAVE YOU ever wondered what it would be like to have access to the pop icons who shape our culture? Personally, I would love to be able to walk out of a movie theater, call up the director, and give him the benefit of my self-appointed critical opinions. Because we are drawn in by the art we experience, we begin to imagine that we are on speaking terms with the individuals who create it.

But you and I can't reach these people. We don't have access. Just *try* to get actor Robert De Niro on the telephone to say that you hated his latest movie. Even if you did get through, how long do you think he would stay on the line once he figured out that it was only plain average *you*?

These people don't *want* us to call them. They surround themselves with layers and layers of insulation. They develop good self-protection instincts and know how to make a hasty exit. All of which makes the following story even more bizarre.

Back in the early 1980s, a curious rumor began to circulate in Hollywood about an elusive woman who called herself "Miranda." She managed to call up and get through to some of the most visible and savvy men of the time, including Robert De Niro, Quincy Jones, Sting, Richard Gere, Warren Beatty, Bob Dylan—even Buck Henry, for heaven's sake!

She was unknown to—and refused to meet—the powerful men she called, yet they took her calls, stayed on the telephone for hours, and hung up looking forward to her next call. According to a well-reported article by Bryan Burrough in the December 1999 issue of *Vanity Fair*, singer Billy Joel tried out new songs on her and sang lyrics into her voice mail. It's even rumored that he sent her a diamond-encrusted Rolex watch. She had proposals of marriage from some of these men. This stuff went on for fifteen years.

Now, you may be thinking that she must have been engaging them in prurient conversation. But according to all reports, that was not the case. She was a little flirty maybe, very charming and rather witty. When she described herself as a slim, blonde, coed heiress, these men believed her. So many of them confided in her that she always had insider gossip to pass along. They were intrigued.

Then one day she suddenly stopped calling. To the embarrassment of many, it was later revealed that Miranda was an overweight social worker from Baton Rouge with a red convertible, a corgi dog, and a large dark mole on her right cheek.

We may never know her motives, but I am fascinated by the way she was able to make these people accept her as being somehow worth their time. Think about it. They had no idea what she looked like. There was only her voice on the telephone. That voice, however, got their full attention. And that is what interests me.

Dress for Success for the Speaking Voice

The people we deal with in life come to know us by the three ways in which we present ourselves: (a) how we look; (b) what we say; and (c) how we say it.

The book *Dress for Success* stressed the importance of how we look. There are shelves of best-selling books to help us with what to say. But when you are talking to your coworkers, your kids, or your cat—or to your kids as they're about to stuff the cat into the blender—often it's how you say it that really counts. Most of us spend years in school learning *what* to say, but little or no time learning *how* to say it. This is alarming, when you realize that *how* we say it is one third of the total impression we make.

Almost every encounter in life depends on our ability to capture and hold the attention of other people. Hollywood stalking may not be our objective, but didn't "Miranda" simply pull off an extreme version of what we hope to do every time we speak? We want people to listen to what we say, to keep on listening, to remember what we say, and maybe, even to act on it.

The voice that represents us must serve us well throughout the day, starting with the way we say "Good morning!"; order breakfast; or yell at other drivers. While you are at work, you are talking on the telephone; meeting with customers, employees, and suppliers; negotiating contracts; talking to your boss; and ordering lunch.

And what if your job or personal interests are voice-intensive, as is the case with teachers and receptionists, salespeople, coaches and sports instructors, dispatchers and telemarketers? Or in situations where it is absolutely crucial to be understood, for example, in surgery—"Give me an IV push of 15 cc's of . . ."; the stock market—

"Sell (cough, cough), I said, SELL, Sell, sell . . ."; or even at your favorite drive-through restaurant—"Darn it! I said *NO* onions! Not *more* onions!" Whether you are on the job, ordering a hamburger, or removing a gallbladder, there is always the potential for chaos when your voice misrepresents you.

The most fundamental power we have for making our lives richer is our ability to communicate—to give voice to our intentions. Oprah Winfrey was right when she said, "Being able to communicate with people is power." When we examine the people in our lives, we see that those who communicate best are the most successful. When we study history, we see that it was shaped by great communicators. When we look at Oprah, we see that the ability to communicate has certainly worked for her. We literally *speak* our lives into being what they are—or what they are not.

We can learn a great deal from singers. Madonna takes the spotlight at center stage, whereas you present your ideas at a client meeting. Both of you must engage and entertain the audience if you want to win them over. When you speak, it is much like becoming the lead singer in your own performance.

Speech is even a form of music. It has tones and timbres, pitches and rhythms. It can be loud or soft, punchy or laid-back, fast or slow. But when you are talking, things are not organized in advance the way they are in a song, so you must improvise on the spot. Speaking is much like singing a song that hasn't been written yet.

My Job

I have a great job—I really do. I'm based in Nashville, and as the voice coach to major recording artists, I'm lucky enough to work with many wonderful singers. It is the perfect job for me because I am absolutely fascinated by the human voice. I've made it my business to learn how to gain control of its functions and to communicate that control to others. Over the years, I have developed my teaching style by getting through to people who you wouldn't think would actually take voice lessons, namely rockers (Bob Weir of the Grateful Dead, Huey Lewis), country stars (Dixie Chicks, Randy Travis, Tim McGraw), and pop singers (Linda Ronstadt, Faith Hill).

Rigors of the studio, ravages of the road, and the stress of performance take a terrible toll on a singer. Today's high-stakes entertainment world is a competitive jungle where survival of the fittest is a constant challenge. A good singer has to be as well prepared as a professional athlete. The entire structure surrounding an artist depends on two little muscles that are less than an inch long, and if those fail, the whole thing crumbles.

In a way, I provide a kind of career protection insurance. Young singers come to me to learn how to develop their tone and find a personal style. Established singers come for new ideas or to clear up a specific problem, perhaps damage brought on by an exhausting tour. Voice training, like physical fitness, is never finished. It's an ongoing necessity.

It's wonderful to see my students take new information and run with it. Sometimes I feel my job is a bit like playing an instrument by remote control. One of my all-time most gratifying moments came while I was walking through the Pittsburgh airport to my connecting flight and heard five songs in a row by five different singers I had coached. I could hear the influence of my work in song after song and it took my breath away. I sat down right there at Gate B4 and cried. But that's what makes me passionate about my work—I love to hear results.

And What Might This Have to Do With Speaking?

Unlike professional singers, most of us take our voices for granted. This is the voice I was born with, so this is the voice I'm stuck with. Well, to a certain extent that is true. But look at it this way: Your hair is the hair you were born with, but that doesn't stop you from wanting to make it look better, does it? Collectively, we spend billions of dollars and untold amounts of energy dealing with hair. Think how much time and money you've spent on your hair in your lifetime. Why not put a little effort into your hardworking, attention-deprived, underappreciated speaking voice?

I've developed techniques for professional singers that will help you to learn more than you might have dreamed possible about solving speaking problems. You'll be surprised how quickly your voice can become more dynamic, effective, and reliable.

What We're Going to Do

This is a proactive program, which is organized into the following four parts:

1. Voice production
2. Techniques for delivery
3. Advice for specific applications
4. Voice survival kit

The challenge here is to communicate concepts that would normally be exchanged in a face-to-face, interactive encounter onto the printed page. You'll come across unusual spellings in this book that indicate a deviation from the way you would normally pronounce a word. Be on the lookout for words in either boldface type or italics, or for words that have extra letters or irregular spacing. Use your imagination as you try to match the sound to the way it reads in print. Say these words aloud several times. Some of the ideas may seem a bit unorthodox—but they work.

In Part I, you'll learn about the techniques of breathing, support, and resonance that will bring out the best qualities in your natural voice. The goal is not to become the next Luciano Pavarotti, but rather to develop a speaking voice that gives you (and others) pleasure to hear. Actress Fran Drescher has made a career out of whining, but would you want her answering the telephones at your law firm?

Part II is the SFX, or special effects, department. An arresting speaker makes good use of color, variety, and surprise. Voice delivery incorporates a wealth of devices—such as rhythm, timing, volume, and the rise and fall of voice pitch—that have a powerful effect on what you say. If you want to learn how to get attention and create drama, this is the part for you.

In Part III, there are special instructions that apply to specific circumstances, including what to do when you're faced with giving a speech, ways in which your voice can affect the outcome of a sales meeting, how to leave a memorable and productive voice mail message, and, ultimately, how to use your voice to get the greatest benefit—with the least amount of hassle—out of your business and personal encounters.

You'll find tips in Part IV for keeping your speaking apparatus healthy and resilient. Take care of your voice and it will serve you long and well. A few survival tactics might even save you some of those days and dollars lost each year to voice-related downtime and doctors' bills.

Just Say No to Latin

I think we all appreciate information that is simple and direct, and concepts that make sense, not something wrapped in mysterious terms that a normal person can't relate to easily. If you are looking for scientific jargon, anatomically correct physiological descriptions, and Latin names for body parts, you're reading the wrong book. "Raise your uvula, dear. . . ." That stuff makes even *my* mind boggle and turn away.

I'll give you images—sometimes physical, sometimes mental—that describe what you should be feeling. Work with them. Be patient. Keep an open mind. Try the exercises in several different ways—things seldom feel exactly the same way to everybody. If I say, "Lift your tongue," that will certainly mean something different to you, and to me, and to everyone else who has a tongue. Experiment, use your imagination, and don't be afraid to exaggerate. Keep your sense of humor and think of the whole picture. If it sounds good and feels good, it probably *is* good.

Voice Nirvana

A technique always works best when it is invisible, that is, when it has become a deeply ingrained habit. And that only happens over time and with plenty of practice. There is a formula for the stages of learning that has been around so long that I don't even know where to give credit. Consider it the four stages on the path to voice nirvana. It looks like this:

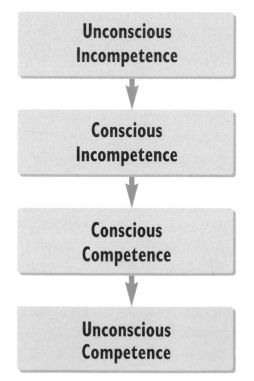

UNCONSCIOUS INCOMPETENCE

Maybe you've never given much thought to *how* you sound or whether there was any prospect of doing anything about it. Having no idea what is wrong or what is possible can be a rather blissful stage.

CONSCIOUS INCOMPETENCE

Here, you are all too aware that improvements could be made. You've learned a few techniques, but they are new and might feel a bit strange. This stage is not much fun.

CONSCIOUS COMPETENCE

You have mastered a host of new skills, but at this stage, you still need to concentrate to keep all the balls in the air.

UNCONSCIOUS COMPETENCE

This is the voice nirvana that we have been working toward. These techniques have become a part of you. You use them without thinking. Technique has set you free.

Cruise Control

It's a lot like driving a car. Driving is a dangerous and potentially life-threatening activity. It is complex. When you first learn how to drive, you need to concentrate on everything you are doing. But after you've been driving a while, you find yourself thinking about other things—your grocery list, dinner, the NASDAQ—and driving settles down to checking in on a few basics, primarily your speed, where you are in your lane, the other cars, turns, and directions. You keep track of safety issues, but your brain handles the mechanics on a kind of "cruise control."

That is what we want to do with voice technique. Explore a few things. Think about them. Practice them. Consciously use them in conversation. Record yourself and listen back. Experiment. Former students of martial arts guru Bruce Lee often quote him as saying, "I cannot teach you. I can only help you explore yourself."

It may take a little work, but how do you get the most out of anything? According to the joke, the same way you get to Carnegie Hall—practice, practice, practice. Whatever you practice stands a good chance of sticking. So stay focused. Practice doesn't make perfect; *perfect* practice makes perfect.

Will this book get you a record deal or onstage at the Metropolitan Opera House? Probably not. It could, however, go a long way toward making your spoken communication more rewarding and your relationships more satisfying and trouble-free. *(But, hey, if you do get a record deal, I'll take all the credit!)*

Rate Your Voice Power

Before we start, let's evaluate your Voice Power quotient. Score yourself on this test once now, then a second time after you have completed this book and have had a chance to put what you've learned into practice.

Would you say that:

Others let you finish talking without interrupting.
　　Always (4) Usually (3) Sometimes (2)
　　Seldom (1) Never (0)　　　　#1 _____　#2 _____

You speak without being asked to repeat yourself.
　　Always (4) Usually (3) Sometimes (2)
　　Seldom (1) Never (0)　　　　#1 _____　#2 _____

People seem to remember what you say.
    Always (4) Usually (3) Sometimes (2)
    Seldom (1) Never (0)   #1 _____   #2 _____

Others are quick to act on your suggestions and commands.
    Always (4) Usually (3) Sometimes (2)
    Seldom (1) Never (0)   #1 _____   #2 _____

You find it easy to change people's minds.
    Always (4) Usually (3) Sometimes (2)
    Seldom (1) Never (0)   #1 _____   #2 _____

At the end of the day your voice still sounds fresh.
    Always (4) Usually (3) Sometimes (2)
    Seldom (1) Never (0)   #1 _____   #2 _____

                    Total #1 _____   #2 _____

If you scored:

    20–24   Have you considered running for office?

    15–19   Your voice is clearly an asset.

    10–14   There is hope, but the competition isn't worried.

    5–9   Ever wonder whether you're invisible?

    0–4   Good luck! You're going to need it.

Next, record yourself reading a short passage or listen to your outgoing message on your answering machine. Take a moment to describe the impression you get from listening to your voice. Write it down. Start by listing three things you found admirable, and then list three qualities that you wish you could change. Be sure to save the recording and your list for comparison later.

CHAPTER TWO

Just Keep Breathing

YOU'RE PROBABLY thinking, *What can she possibly tell me about breathing? Inhale, exhale, repeat, right?*

Every couple of years in the world of sports training, a new device or technique turns up that gives athletes a competitive edge—and is actually legal. This year's buzz word might be "miracle suiting," next year it might be "carbo-packing" or "high-altitude workouts." Recently, a special body-efficient method of breathing that helps an athlete to conserve energy has become a hot trend in sports fitness. It is widely used to boost endurance and cut fatigue in training programs for runners, cyclists, and swimmers.

This breathing method goes by many different names, including reverse breathing, upside-down breathing, breathplay, and the no-breathing breathing. Since the common denominator is relaxed, unlabored, natural breathing that requires little effort, I use the term *passive breathing*.

You might wonder, *Well, that may make sense for sports. Personally, I seem to be doing just fine.* If you are reading this chapter, clearly you've figured something out about breathing because you're alive, but what about the way you breathe when you speak?

When we speak, we force breath through our vocal cords. The cords vibrate and produce a tone, much like whistling through two blades of grass. Speech is a complex play of brain, body, and voice—an athletic event involving strength, endurance, control, and flexibility—issues similar to those that concern sports professionals. Speaking is a marvel of small-muscle athletics. And like sports, it all starts with the breath. You've got to *move* some air.

As we breathe, the large thin muscle resting beneath our lungs, which is called the diaphragm *(not a Latin word)* relaxes and flattens downward, creating a vacuum. Air flows in to fill the space. When the diaphragm contracts, the air is exhaled back out. The whole thing works like a giant turkey baster. Air in. Air out.

Sounds pretty simple doesn't it? So, what is the big deal about breathing? Think how often we breathe—on average, at least every six seconds or so, which makes ten times a minute, *600 times an hour!* Who knows how many times a day, a week, a month, or a year? You would think it would be difficult for something we do so often to go wrong. Still, it manages to confound a great number of us.

Breathing Gone Bad

What is breathing gone bad? We see signs of it in ourselves and in others around us—the shallow-breathers, the chest-heavers, and the gaspers. It is breathing that limits the control we have over our bodies, our brains, and the voice we use to speak. It saps our energy. It puts us on edge and strangles our sound.

On the other hand, passive breathing is as relaxed and easy as falling down a drain. Literally. You simply open up your throat and let the air fall in, like water going down an open drain. It's the way we breathed as children—before things got complicated.

The Breathalyzer Test

What type of breather are you? Let's find out. Round up the following household items: a body-length mirror, a chair, and a tape recorder. And should there be a spare turkey baster lying around, grab that too. If you are currently in an aisle seat, cruising along at an altitude of 28,000 feet, or soaking in the tub, just use your imagination now and check your results later with the mirror and tape recorder.

Bring this book with you and stand in front of the mirror so that we can analyze where you're starting out. Get ready to take a deep breath, paying close attention to what happens to your mouth, shoulders, and chest. Okay, inhale. What did you see? Do it a few more times.

What happened, exactly? First, did you take the air in through your nose or through your mouth? Second, where did you stash the air you took in? Did your chest expand or your shoulders rise? And third, how would you say the air got from the *outside* of your body to the *inside* of your body? Suppose you had to describe the process to aliens, or fish, or something else that couldn't relate to human breathing. Would you say that you drew it in, pulled it in, or sucked it in?

THE ROUTE

Some breathing methods advocate breathing through the nose, but not this one. Although it is not a bad way to breathe, there are reliability issues. What do you do if you suffer from sinus or allergy conditions? Not breathe at all during ragweed season? Because there isn't much point in learning a technique you can't count on, I teach breathing through the mouth. If some air does come in through your nose as well, consider it a welcome bonus.

THE DESTINATION

Next, I had asked you to notice where you put your air. Most likely, you breathed into your chest and then filled up around your shoulders. If you saw your midsection expand instead, that's good. But I'd like to suggest that you direct the air even lower. In fact, the point to aim for is right below your waist. Put your thumb on your navel and walk your fingers down an inch or two. That's the spot.

THE MEANS

Now, instead of drawing, pulling, or sucking the air in, I'm going to show you how to open up, create a space, and just let the air *fall* in. Imagine a tube going straight down your throat that ends in a little air sack at your lower abdominal area.

And yes, I understand that there are no lungs down there. There is, however, a drop in the diaphragm muscle that manifests itself in the lower abdominal area so that it *looks* and *feels* as though we're putting air down there. So, when I talk about it, I'm going to say, "Breathe into your lower abdominals," even though there are no actual lung parts down there.

The Path to Passive Breathing

The first step in learning passive breathing starts with the exhale. Hold your fist right below your navel. Now, exactly at the spot where your fist is, isolate and flex only those lower abdominal muscles and squeeze out a little puff of air. Not from your waist, but rather from below your waist, or down by your fist. But only a little air. Imagine that you are a giant turkey baster. Squeeze the air out of the bottom of the bulb.

To let the air back in again, picture yourself hollow below the waist. Let your lower abdominal muscles relax as you loosen your jaw and open your throat, as if you were yawning. Keep your throat relaxed and open so that the air can flow in. Visualize about a fistful of air falling directly down to the bottom of your torso.

Now squeeze the air back out again with a light grip from your lower abdominal muscles. And *voilà!* You're breathing!

Stop! Go back and read the previous three paragraphs one more time.

The process should work as easily as my favorite teaching tool— the lowly turkey baster. When you squish the bulb flat, you push the air out. When you release the bulb, air falls back in. But notice that when you block the opening of the turkey baster, it doesn't matter what you do with the bulb because the air can't get in. There has to be an opening. Your throat is analogous to this opening. Make certain that it stays open.

I encourage you to relax your jaw as you practice this. Open wide. Let the back of your tongue drop down. Find your Adam's apple and let it drop, too. But feel your uvula—that thing way back in your throat that Tom and Jerry hang onto in cartoons—lift. (*Okay, there was a Latin word.*) Try it again. Squeeze—air out. Open—air in.

Human Balloon

You don't have to take big breaths. Filling your lungs with air is like filling up a balloon—only you're the balloon. After you blow up a balloon, you have to pinch it off at the neck or the air is going to whoosh right back out. Now picture yourself as a large, rather ungainly balloon. What do you have to do to your throat when you take a large breath? You're forced to tighten it to keep the air from escaping.

I suggest never filling beyond your resting capacity because beyond that point your throat has to constrict, which cuts off the flexibility and resonance of your voice. The more air you force in and hold, the more it tightens.

If you took voice lessons or played in your high school band, you may have been taught to breathe in all the air you can and to keep your chest expanded while you perform. As a conservatory-trained classical singer, I encountered this during a summer when I studied with a flute teacher from Oakland, California. She was considered a breathing specialist in the Bay Area. Breathing *torture* specialist was more like it.

She made me wear a belt midway around my rib cage, instructing me to keep my ribs expanded against it the entire time I sang— even when I was out of air. Now, does that make any sense? It's like asking a tire to stay inflated after the air is all gone. Where's the logic?

Think what you are doing to your throat when you fill up and make speaking sounds by gradually releasing the death grip on your neck. It's like that other thing you can do with a balloon. You know how you can blow up a balloon, stretch the neck sideways, and let out a little air? There is a high-pitched squeal as the air escapes. It goes *eeeeee!* Can this possibly be good for your voice?

Ebb and Flow

Besides, there is no need to replace all the air in our lungs each time we breathe, only some of it—the 35 percent that is called *tidal* air. According to *Compton's Encyclopedia,* "Air that flows in and out of the lungs as we breathe is called the tidal volume because it increases and decreases in a regular rhythm like the ocean tides." The remaining 65 percent is residual air that is left in the lungs to prevent them from collapsing.

Let's review passive breathing once more to be certain that it is making sense to you. This time, try relaxing in a chair or even lying down. Find that spot again, by putting your thumb at your navel and measuring down a couple of inches. The goal is to keep the air low and as far away from your throat as possible. Relax your chest. Now contract and squeeze out about a fistful of air (*Exhale*). Relax even more and let the same amount fall back in, straight down into your lower body (*Inhale*).

Make certain that you release those muscles quickly. There is not much time between sentences so you have to train your abdominal muscles to release instantaneously, and that can be a little scary for people. The concept of relaxed abdominal muscles doesn't exactly reconcile with our Western standards of beauty, and some of us really resist letting go down there.

If we're carrying a few extra pounds around the middle, we tend to harbor the unrealistic notion that we'll remember to hold our stomachs in. If the last thing that you do before leaving the house is to take a look in the mirror and suck your stomach in, try to get over that habit. Nobody can keep that up for hours. We're not fooling anybody. We have to lose those pounds through exercise and diet—they won't disappear by sucking in. Don't let vanity keep you from relaxing your abdominal muscles while you practice.

Now Picture This

Remember, the objective in passive breathing is to simply let the air fall in like water going down a drain. Picture a kitchen sink half full of water from a cross-sectional side view. It has one of those flat rubber pads your grandmother used to have, blocking the drain. What happens when you pull the plug? The water just drains right down.

It makes sense, doesn't it? If you were underwater and decided for some reason to open up your mouth and throat, what would happen? The water would rush in. Right? Well, air will do the same thing. You don't have to pull it in, suck it in, or actively breathe it in. Simply create a vacuum. Nature abhors a vacuum. And wherever you create a space for it, air will automatically flow in, without any effort on your part—*because it can!*

Breathing is quite uncomplicated when you think of it this way. Actually, the hardest part about passive breathing is that it *is* so simple. It is difficult to keep things simple, but "simple" can be very effective. The popular phrase "Keep it simple, stupid (KISS)" didn't become an over-invoked acronym by accident.

Once, I attempted to be more scientific about what happens to the lungs during passive breathing, so I taught it to my doctor hoping that he would give me an official physiological explanation. When we were finished, all he said was, "I have no idea what's going on, but I hope I breathe this way the rest of my life." (*Did I mention that he's a saxophone player?*)

This is the way we breathed as infants. Find yourself an infant, or better yet, go look at a batch of them lined up in the observation room of a maternity ward and you'll see that they breathe naturally from their tummies. Of course, an infant who is crying or upset will tend to hyperventilate up in the chest, but at rest they normally breathe very low.

We probably stopped breathing this way at around age four when somebody dragged us in front of a mirror and started scolding: "Chest out! Shoulders back! Stomach in!" Who wouldn't be tense? I'm a big fan of good posture, but you can carry yourself well without filling up your lungs. Passive breathing may take a little more trust in the beginning, especially if you miss the power hit of pressure that a big breath gives you up in the chest, but it will feel much better in the long run and the amount of air that falls in will be sufficient—I promise.

Freedom of Voice

What happens to your voice when you don't breathe into your lower body? Shallow breathing makes you sound breathy and weak. Tension around the neck stiffens the vocal cords, making them rigid, unresponsive, and vulnerable to damage. It cuts off the resonance and reduces resilience and flexibility. The pitch rises. You feel *and* sound strangled. In short, you sound uptight. Why do you think it's called *uptight*? I've never heard anyone accused of being *down*tight.

You'll get a richer, fuller voice with low abdominal breathing because your body and vocal cords are free to vibrate. Reducing the pressure at your throat can increase resonance so that your voice will project with power, even under adverse conditions. Also, what you say is important, but we'll never hear all of it if you keep running out of air. Passive breathing puts more air at your disposal so that you don't run out of breath before you run out of words.

Extra Value Added

The speaking mechanism is a complex and interdependent system. All the parts—body, brain, and voice—affect the whole. I'm especially intrigued by the benefits of passive breathing that go beyond those normally associated with speaking.

For Your Body

CARDIOVASCULAR

Wait until you discover how passive breathing improves your performance during a cardiovascular workout. The logic is that if you are moving fast and don't have to work as hard at breathing, you'll have more stamina and energy for action. Why waste precious energy pulling air into your lungs when you can let physics do the work and simply let it fall in?

When I changed over to this breathing, I was teaching aerobics classes five or six days a week, so I was in fairly good shape already. Overnight (and I do mean *overnight*), I became the "Aerobics Teacher from Hell," driving each class to exhaustion because suddenly I could go on and on forever. Even the students who used to keep up with me began falling out. I found I had to incorporate a breathing pattern into all my classes so that they wouldn't go into cardiac arrest. Eat my dust, Energizer Bunny!

PULSE RATE

Once I actually lowered my pulse rate during a fitness test just to see whether I could do it. At the start of a fitness test, they usually take your resting pulse and then have you run around for three to five minutes before recording your pulse again to find out how much it has accelerated. By using passive breathing, I could drop my pulse rate down a few notches from where it had started. It really confused the bewildered test monitor. She looked at me strangely, but figured she had made a mistake and wrote down "normal."

MUSCLE TONE WITH WEIGHTS

If you include weights in your exercise program, do the hardest part while exhaling, then inhale on the rebound. For example, during a bench press, exhale on the lift and inhale as you release downward. For sit-ups, exhale as you lift your body and inhale when you lower yourself back to the floor. Breathing from your lower abdominal muscles helps to keep the primary resistance centered low, generating power from the strongest part of your body. Even a biceps curl can be done using lower abdominal resistance. Squeeze the air out with your lower abdominal muscles, pushing in as you lift.

MULTITASKING DURING EXERCISE

Perhaps, like me, you find boredom to be a barrier to regular exercise. There are only so many ways to get excited about counting to eight—*again*. However, it can be a great opportunity for practicing your breathing skills. You're already in a state of concentration. It gives you something to think about. And a strong sense of rhythm always makes exercise more pleasurable and hypnotic. Incorporate breathing into the rhythm pattern and your workout becomes more like dancing—only with weights.

Passive breathing will help keep your body toned, your heart rate and blood pressure low, your body centered, and your energy up so that you will always be at the top of your game. At the very least, it is a subtle, but persistent, lower abdominal exerciser in itself. All those contractions down there are bound to tighten your *entire* lower body.

NECK AND SHOULDER TENSION

Do you ever find that you have tension in your neck and shoulders? Who doesn't? Just think about those 600 or so breaths we take each hour, as we clench and unclench our throat muscles to control the flow. No wonder we're tense. Passive breathing, on the other hand, does all the work way down in the lower body, so that your neck and shoulders can relax. Personally, I would rather be contracting and releasing my lower abdominal muscles—toning the muscles I really want to tone.

The body consumes oxygen (O) and releases carbon dioxide (CO_2) into the bloodstream as a waste by-product. Air that is bottled up around your neck reduces the blood flow and prevents the elimination of toxic wastes—a frequent source of headaches for many people. A part of our central nervous system called the sympathetic nervous system becomes active when we breathe into the upper chest, and contributes to high blood pressure, accelerated heart rate, feelings of panic, and increased risk of heart attacks. We are literally choking ourselves.

The next time tension starts creeping in, use the breathing technique you've just learned. As you find alternative muscles in your lower body, upper body tension starts to disappear. You will be more productive during the day and more relaxed at the end of it if you make time for breathing breaks. At the end of this chapter, you'll find a two-minute StressBuster that you can use whenever you feel the need to refresh and revive. You'll find it especially useful when those afternoon doldrums hit.

CENTER OF GRAVITY

Your personal center of gravity is located wherever you direct your breath. Have you ever known someone who was normal in every other way, but seemed to be naturally clumsy? I've had friends who could trip over things that weren't even there. Their own two feet were like strangers.

I've noticed these people have a tendency to breathe high, far away from the geographical center of their bodies. Being top-heavy, they're easily thrown off-balance when they have to change direction. Breathe low into your body and your personal center of gravity will be centered where it should be.

BIRTH OF A BACKACHE

Off-center breathing puts your back at risk for injury whenever you lift or move a heavy load. Martial arts enthusiasts rely on low breathing to focus the seat of balance and power at the dead center of their bodies—all power radiates outward from there. Passive breathing, with its low center of gravity, will help you engage muscles from the strongest part of your body—those in your lower body, legs, hips, upper thighs—thereby protecting your back from possible injury, whether you're saving the dojo from the bad guys or simply rearranging the furniture.

And should you be called upon to catch something with little or no warning, you're more likely to use muscles from the strongest part of your body if you have a low center of gravity. Suppose you suddenly had to catch a child tumbling out of a tree house, would you be balanced and ready to respond with strength from the center of your body, or off-balance and headed for a back brace? Save the child. Save the day. Save your back. You're a Superhero.

For Your Brain

RETURN TO CENTER

Once a student asked me how to "center" himself before a big performance. Although I realized he was asking how to prepare himself mentally, his question made me reexamine a term we use frequently without considering all of its meanings. Doesn't centering also carry the implication that you should direct the breath toward the center of your body, below your waist?

Passive breathing, with its emphasis on centering, relaxes you, almost inducing a light state of meditation. During this time of concentration, your brain is like a blank sheet of paper, ready to focus your mental powers on the matter at hand. You are better able to separate the important from the extraneous because you have a clear mind with which to approach your challenges.

The ability to focus is one of the most powerful tools possessed by those who succeed in their endeavors. It is often said that successful people are an inch wide and a mile deep because they delve deeply into one chosen subject or field, and their willingness to focus makes them a valued player in that field. However, people who are scattered a mile wide and an inch deep rarely seem to parlay that strategy into success.

Rx FOR STRESS

Anxiety is another by-product of a cluttered mind. Generally, worrying about all your problems at the same time won't do much to solve them. However, by focusing your mind, you are better able to knock them off one by one. An unsettled mind paralyzes your ability to act in a way that best serves your interests—*(the wheel is turning, but the hamster is in a coma).*

Passive breathing relaxes you, lowers your blood pressure, and calms your nerves so that you are more likely to keep your cool in volatile situations. The next time you feel yourself drawn into a bout of road rage, try a dose—it just may keep you out of jail. Indeed, I prescribe passive breathing as a home remedy for many of the anxieties we face on a daily basis—fear, anger, stress, the blues, performance anxiety, stage fright—whatever gives you the jitters. It's free, it's fast, and you don't have to argue with your HMO.

For most of us, relaxation is a good thing, but I guess there will always be at least one exception. And in this case, that would be Alice. Alice was a well-known Nashville songwriter who came to me for voice lessons so that she could sing her own demos. Alice was wrapped pretty tight. Okay, she was a bundle of energy and was wrapped *way* too tight. It took her longer to learn passive breathing than anyone I can remember, but she worked hard at it, and after five lessons she finally mastered it.

She showed up at her next lesson insisting, "Renee, this just isn't working for me." I was shocked because she had come so far, and so I asked her what she meant. "It's relaxing me too much. I'm losing my edge." For her, I think, the edge was way up on a cliff somewhere. There is clearly no way to please everyone. I guess she found a channel for all that energy and edge a few years later. It was Alice Randall who conceived and authored the highly controversial, much-litigated *Gone With the Wind* parody entitled *The Wind Done Gone.*

Practice Makes Perfect

Old habits don't die easily. Together, we must convince your body that it is okay to breathe like this all the time. Passive breathing will become useful to you only when it has become second nature. And to change something as basic as breathing, you must devote some time to it. But that doesn't mean you have to stand in front of the mirror all day. Incorporate it into your life.

Think about it and use it when you are in the shower, when you are making a cup of coffee, or when you are brushing your teeth. Practice while you are waiting for a left-turn signal or when you are on hold on the telephone—whenever and wherever you can. Put up signs, put up Post-it Notes to remind you. Teach it to your friends. The fastest way to learn anything is to try explaining it to another person—you end up learning more yourself by finding a way to make it clear to someone else.

You have an opportunity to retrain your body to breathe in a *new* way—one that meets the needs not only of athletes or singers but of everyone who uses his voice to speak. Return to it hundreds of times each day until it becomes part of you. Become obsessed for a couple of weeks and it will stay with you forever. This is unconscious competence, or voice nirvana.

Two-Minute StressBuster

Here is a short energy break designed to relax, focus, and energize you. I call it the two-minute StressBuster—a simple breathing technique that can help take the stress out of your day, while giving your body and brain a boost when you need it most.

Sit comfortably with your body as relaxed as possible, your hands open at your sides, and your chin dropped down toward your chest. This can be done standing up when there are no other options, but the less tension in your body position, the better. Close your eyes. Imagine opening up your throat and opening the space below your waist. Let the air fall in.

Hover there for just a brief moment. Don't actually hold your breath. Just pause ever so briefly before you gently contract to exhale. Let your body slump a little more each time. Gradually allow more and more space between breaths as you relax more deeply with each cycle.

Think only of that gentle expand/contract pattern. Let the air come in through your mouth or nose, or both if you like, whatever is comfortable for you. Take in only a small amount of air—never filling beyond your resting capacity. Feel the breath drop into your lower abdominal area. Imagine water going down a drain. Focus your concentration on the act of breathing.

Continue this for at least two minutes. Sometimes that is all the time you have, but don't feel that you must limit yourself to two minutes. Longer is better. Twenty minutes is ideal, but even a short StressBuster break will go a long way toward relaxing you— bringing your body and mind back into focus.

A Sound Foundation

IS THERE anyone out there who can honestly say that they have never fallen into a quick Elvis imitation—not even *once*?

We all know what to do. Go into a karate-type crouch. Kind of hunker down and drop your head. Give us a sultry look and put a little shake, rattle, and roll in your shoulders. It was the Elvis trademark and it was very sexy.

But did Elvis do it just to be sexy? Maybe not. One day I was working with country great Tim McGraw; we were positioning his support for the first time when he looked up with a little mischief in his eyes and mumbled in true Elvis-fashion, *"Thank you. Thankyouverymuch."*

I suddenly saw that the techniques I had been teaching my students for years were mirrored in Elvis's signature moves. Those classic heart-stopping, hip-shaking gyrations weren't only sexy—they made him a better singer.

Elvis used strong legs as his power base, keeping a wide stance and pushing into the floor, while his upper body stayed loose and resonant. Rounding his head over the microphone helped his voice vibrate and ring. I'm certain even the curl of his lip and the intense smoldering look were somehow involved. Say what you will about his lifestyle, the man kept his voice until the end. He must have been doing something right.

Was Elvis aware of the specific techno-physio-scientific dynamics of his vocal technique? Probably not. I think, though, that in his own way he truly studied singing. He used to sit out on the back porch for hours on late summer nights with the guitar his mother had bought him, trying to imitate the singers he heard when he sneaked out to the gospel churches and nightclubs across town.

As he experimented, Elvis did whatever it took to wring the sound he wanted from himself, persisting until he found the moves that turned him into the perfect singing machine. Of course, it was a sign of his genius that instead of downplaying these physical aspects, he had the courage to make them his personal signature. At least, that's my theory.

I freely admit I look to him for "singin' " tips, so there are quite a few great singers out there now using concepts that come straight from "The King." I think my students are surprised and grateful to have something familiar to lock on to. Those moves register as good solid voice technique and it soon starts making sense: "Hey, if Elvis did it, it must be cool."

Now, I don't necessarily want you to speak like Elvis spoke, but

I do hope you'll speak like he *sang*, with warmth, flexibility, and a richness of tone destined to be remembered long after you've "left the building."

Support and Resonance

With Elvis as our guide, we turn our attention to the next two building blocks of voice technique—support and resonance.

The system of muscles that collectively produce a speaking sound is called *support*. Its companion is *resonance*, which is the way the sound then vibrates in the body. Support and resonance work together in a delicate balance. It takes power to support the tone, yet we must draw that power from a source that does not compromise its resonance.

The human body, like any other vibrating instrument, must be relaxed and loose to resonate freely. We truly are instruments. Like a gong that vibrates when it is struck, every part of us vibrates when we speak, down to the last quivering eyebrow. Touching a gong stops the vibrations and dampens the sound, just as the wrong kind of pressure dampens the resonance in a voice.

But speaking takes energy. Like a lump of coal waiting for fire to transform it into heat, your body requires an explosion of power to transfer its latent energy into sound. And that power must come from somewhere. It's not merely a question of saying, "Oh, hey— just relax." It's a question of developing a substitute source of power that doesn't involve your neck and throat. Picture the classic Elvis stance. Strong legs and a loose upper body gave him both power and freedom. I call it full-body support.

Get ready to use your body in some new and unexpected ways. It might be useful to try things out both sitting and standing. We are going back to the same low muscles we used to breathe. If you are uncertain as to whether you've conquered passive breathing, take another look at Chapter 2.

The Fast Track to Full-Body Support

Start by relocating the spot where you put your breath. Place your fist directly below your navel. Squeeze the old air out, relax your jaw, open up your throat, and pop in a small supply of new air.

Now press in with your fist and contract your lower abdominal muscles *around* the air as you make this short buzzy sound—**ZZ**. Actually feel the buzz start down there instead of in your throat or mouth—**ZZ**. Stay completely relaxed above the waist. It should feel like a **ZZ** is climbing up your zipper. **ZZZZZZZZZZZZ**.

To stop the **ZZ**, relax your abdominal muscles; open up; let in a new puff of air. And, *voilà!*, you're ready for the next one!

Wait! Go back through the previous three paragraphs one more time.

Make certain that the **ZZ** is a buzzy sound. It's not like pronouncing the letter **Z**; it's a buzz, more like a sound that you would hear coming from your weed eater. (*I won't go near weed eaters since the night I dreamed mine was not a vegetarian.*)

Let's try this again. Hunker down like you're cruising along on a Harley. Relax your chest. Tuck your hips under you. Think "laid-back." Flex your muscles around the air again as you tuck under—**ZZ**.

Now repeat the **ZZ** several times, letting the buzz sounds flow together: **ZZ—ZZ—ZZ**. Relax your throat. Gently contract the *surface* of your lower abdominal muscles to make the sound repeat: **ZZ—ZZ—ZZ**. One more time. Tuck your hips slightly under your body as if you were about to lift something heavy: **ZZ—ZZ—ZZ**.

If you think of the word *support* in the broader sense, support usually refers to something that is under something else. You might lift a light chair with one arm, but if it's the Barca-Lounger or the La-Z-Boy you're lifting, that would be a different story. You have to put the weight of your body behind it. Imagine a heavier, richer voice that needs to be hefted just like a heavier chair. You're going to need some power under you.

It's okay to feel tension in your lower body—the good kind of tension, which is power. Tension is not always a pejorative term. The tension in a rubber band gives it strength, and tension in our muscles makes us move. We use this type of tension to speak, but our goal is to keep it as far away from the throat as possible.

EE-I-EE-I-OH

Stick with the **ZZ**s until you're confident that you're feeling the correct sensations and can find them on command. Put that buzzing sensation into a kind of muscle memory to use as a guide. Now, let's try a different sound: **EE**. Then try, **EE—EE—EE**. Let everything contract into the center of your body. Balance on the balls of your feet and press into the floor with the strength of your legs and lower body under you. *(This might be a good time to go into one of those Elvis imitations.)* **EE—EE—EE**. If you're doing it correctly, you should feel a strong buzzing sensation in your lower abdominal muscles.

Try some other sounds. Start with a few simple letters: **NN—NN—NN**; **AH—AH—AH**; **MM—MM—MM**. Remember, pressure in your jaw will thin out the sound, so be sure your jaw is relaxed: **OH—OH—OH**; **VV—VV—VV**. Keep reestablishing the sensations. Admittedly, the sounds that best identify these sensations are a little dorky—don't be surprised if they resemble sound effects normally associated with gardening tools, kitchen appliances, ghosts, and barnyard animals.

Always drop back on your hips and keep your chest loose, your legs and lower body will compensate by tightening under you. If you notice, singers like Celine Dion, Christina Aguilera, Faith Hill, and Natalie Maines of the Dixie Chicks all support from the center of their bodies. A good crunch in the middle gives a singer power. Size doesn't matter. Look at Christina. She's just a slip of a thing—barely 5'2"—but she packs a wallop.

Develop a habit of exhaling first to get rid of the old air so you'll be ready to start with a fresh supply. Breathe low—wherever you put the air into your body is where you'll press to push it back out. If you start to lose the buzz in your lower body, go back to the **ZZ** sounds until you recover it.

Resonance on the Brain

Elvis embodied the essence of resonance. When he cocked his head over the microphone he was helping the sound spin up in his head, just one of the things that gave his voice its rich, warm quality. If you were doing your Elvis imitation, you wouldn't stretch your neck back—that strangles the sound. You would arch your head over and direct the sound up toward your brain.

You may be as surprised as I was to learn that the brain is the single most resonant area of the body. I had no idea that was the case until I was told so by a friend who was completing his doctorate in the physiology of sound. I said, "Wait a minute, isn't that just a bunch of squishy stuff up there?" "Yes," he agreed, "but haven't you ever thumped a watermelon?"

He went on to tell me that the biological makeup of the human head is very close to that of a watermelon. Both do, indeed, contain squishy stuff surrounded by a semihard organic shell. Both are resonant in a melon-y sort of way.

Subtle changes in positioning affect the resonance of your voice. Try the following exercise to hear how sound is affected by merely altering the angle of your head. Hold your head in a normal position and whistle. Now, tilt your head back, look up at the ceiling, and try whistling again. Do you hear what happens? The sound strangles off, losing its resonance when you tilt back.

Okay, no one looks straight up at the ceiling while they're speaking, but you can hear how there is a relationship between the way you hold your head and the way the sound resonates. Try not to lead with your chin as you speak. Instead, arch your whole head slightly forward so that the sound is free to resonate.

The Sweet Spot

Now, what about Elvis's famous lip curl? Where does it fit in? I'm convinced that it was also instrumental in creating his sound. Elvis was known for his warm, resonant tone, but there was always an edge to his voice as well—a strong focal point that put spin and signature on it. I think the lip curl helped him find that edge.

As sound leaves your body it needs to resonate against something specific. You have options—you can direct that flow of sound to the nose, the throat, the jaw, or to the sinus cavities in the face, often called the mask. But I think the best place to aim the vibration stream is right at your teeth. That's right. Your teeth. You'll find a kind of sweet spot at the front of your teeth where you can focus vibrations and still pick up resonance from all these other areas. I'll show you how to find that spot, but you're going have to use a little imagination—*and* everything else you've learned about breathing and support.

The Road to Resonance

Relax the tip of your tongue and gently press the sides up against the ridges behind your teeth. Using support, say: **ZZ**. Make it buzz where your tongue meets your teeth: **ZZ—ZZ—ZZ**.

Don't tighten your jaw. Keep your throat and upper body loose, but remember to tuck under and support with your lower body.

The amount of pressure on your abdominal muscles should equal the pressure at your teeth. Again, **ZZ—ZZ—ZZ**. And, *voilà!*, it's all working together!

Okay. Go back and run through the previous three paragraphs once again.

Here's where the lip curl comes in. If you curl your upper lip a little, you can feel and hear the sound buzz more easily. Try it: **ZZ—ZZ—ZZ**. Create a balance of equal and opposite pressure between your teeth and your support as you buzz. Then experiment with some of the other sounds we've just used. With the **ZZ** sensation as a guide, practice buzzing the following sounds in your teeth: **EE—EE—EE; AA—AA—AA; AH—AH—AH; OH—OH—OH; OO—OO—OO**.

Buzz Words

When you feel that you can keep the buzz going on single sounds, experiment with short words, such as *no, yes, right, now, run,* and *zest.* Then, in like groups of three: *run, ran, rain; that, these, those;* and *have, heart, start.* Once you have a grip on the way support and resonance work together, you can make other sounds—and, eventually, *all* the sounds you want.

Practice so that you can graduate to entire sentences without losing the buzz in your teeth. Start with short phrases and gradually expand to longer, more complete sentences. Use lower body support so you never feel tightness in your throat. Try the classic line from *My Fair Lady,* "The rain in Spain stays mainly in the plain," and notice how your support kicks in to help those **NN**s vibrate in your teeth instead of in your throat. Make up a rap version. Be creative and have some fun with it. Anything that keeps you interested. Keep on building and extending your rap lines. Bust a move!

If you make it part of your life, you will soon be supporting and resonating everything you say. Always start with passive breathing. Check in frequently to make certain that you remember to use support. Keep feeling that buzz sensation the entire time. Record yourself so you can hear the differences and track your progress. Stay loose and think of Elvis.

Visualize This

Now let's talk about another Elvis trademark—those hooded eyes. Or should we call it focus instead? I choose to believe that he was "taking care of business" and concentrating on his voice. Even Elvis had to have an idea of what he wanted to hear in order to reproduce it.

The best singers, like Linda Ronstadt, are always looking to improve their craft. Ronstadt continues to reinvent herself—trying new ideas and pushing the envelope with her voice. Think of how many styles she has successfully explored. She has had a folk career, a rock career, and a punk period. She recorded songs from Hispanic folklore, was on Broadway in *Pirates of Penzance*, and made big band recordings with Nelson Riddle that are timeless. Her voice is always appropriate to the style, yet always clearly Linda.

The first time we worked together, she really caught me off-guard. I was naturally more than a little nervous about being asked to find something to teach one of my heroes. We got started. I gave her an exercise to sing and she just stared at me. For what seemed like a *really long* time. I mean, a *really* long time. She kept staring. Of course my brain was racing, "She thinks this is nuts. She thinks I'm nuts. She's trying to come up with a safe way to get out of the room."

Then she did the exercise and executed it very well. Okay, I thought, so far, so good. So I gave her another exercise to sing. Same thing. I came to realize that she was taking time to form the sound in her mind before she sang it. Then, like pushing the Play button, she simply reproduced it. She didn't just guess. She had to picture it first, taste it, and know how it would feel *and* sound. I was very impressed.

The Good, the Bad, and the Ugly

We have choices when we speak. Imagine your ideal voice. Close your eyes. What do you want to sound like? Who do you like to listen to? Start listening closely to other voices. What qualities do you admire? Pick someone you might want to sound like. The act of choosing will make you examine voices in an entirely different way.

Some box-office giants are known for the career-making qualities of their voices. Sean Connery has a voice that announces, "I am a powerful, intelligent, in-control, good-looking man." You don't have to see him to know it. Julia Roberts' voice registers warmth, beauty, humor, and accessibility. Her voice clearly indicates that she is comfortable with who she is. These two actors are at the top of their field and represent the box-office ideal for their gender. Even with the picture off, we can hear something special there.

Visualize what you want to hear, then you can almost *think* your way into the voice you want. Yes, you use different voices for different situations, but you're always uniquely *you*. The tough part is to decide what you want your voice to say about you. Once you've made a conscious decision, it's not difficult to manipulate the forces involved. If you can visualize it, you can recreate it. But you have to be able to visualize it first. Then breathing, support, and resonance techniques come into play to help execute it. Perception becomes reality.

The Wind Beneath Your Words

I came to see how important this was when I worked with Gary Morris, who made his mark as Jean Valjean in *Les Misérables* on Broadway, and with the original hit of "Wind Beneath My Wings." One night over dinner I asked him how he related to the audience in a performance. Where did he direct his voice? Did he sing to the general audience? Did he focus on one person in the audience? Did he sing to someone in the front row? To the people in the back row?

We chatted about my question for a while, then he became quiet a moment before confiding, "And you know, Renee, sometimes I sing just because I love to hear the sound of my own voice." It was thrilling he answered that way, and you can hear it in his singing. He just *puts* it out there because he loves what he hears. It's a wonderful thing.

How do *you* feel when you listen to yourself? Is your voice an asset or a liability? In Chapter 1, you listed some of the qualities you noticed. Congratulations if you had the following qualities on your list:

* Rich and full
* Mellow and soothing
* Warm and sincere
* Clear and precise
* Commanding
* In control

When your voice is under control, you keep people focused on what you say because there is nothing to distract from the words and the sentiments behind them. But what if any of the following terms describe what you heard on your recording?

* Whispery and raspy
* Nasally and thin
* Shallow and insincere
* Whiny and grating
* Squeaky and pinched
* Out-of-control

Could you be sending the wrong messages—putting the brakes on your career and bringing unwelcome distress into your life?

Kudos if none of these qualities describes the way you sound under normal circumstances, but are you sure they don't creep in when you're tired, cranky, upset, nervous, or called upon to speak in public? Passive breathing and full-body support will help you to control your voice and give you the means to manipulate the tone to suit every situation you may encounter.

To project the image that represents you best, your voice must come from your entire body—if you speak only from your throat, you will never be taken seriously. I recommend that you make a conscious effort to breathe low, support your sound, keep your resonating areas free and loose, and have a good clear image of the voice you want to hear. But like Linda and Elvis, you must begin by visualizing what you want to hear, so why not shoot for the voice of your dreams?

delivery
techniques

The Amazing Power of Consonants

SOME TIME ago, a young singer walked into my Nashville voice studio for a consultation—and I must say, he looked great. He was tall, handsome, had the perfect chin dimple, and melted into his jeans. He really looked like a "singin' " star.

But the high-wattage smile and winning manner couldn't disguise his frustration. He had been in Nashville three years and didn't understand why none of the record labels had signed him to a major record deal. Just looking at him, I was pretty surprised myself.

So, I asked to hear him sing. He had a fine natural voice. He sang in tune and his rhythm was good. It was all very pleasant, but before long, I found myself drifting off—adding items to my grocery list. He was *not* holding my attention.

Now that is a serious problem for a singer. Mr. Dimple had a good voice and he looked good, but this guy could have been arrested for loitering in front of a band. There was definitely something missing. It really made me think.

That same summer, a management firm brought me another young singer who made a completely different impression. He was friendly and sincere looking—like someone you would trust with your X rays or who might help you get your car running again. No movie star dimple. No flowing locks. And the jeans? Not bad, but you could see that wrestling with his weight might be an ongoing concern. Nothing about him hinted that he could be a major country star, although the management team that sent him was a good one and they certainly believed in him. I, however, didn't get it.

As soon as I heard him sing, though, I *did* get it. He didn't have the perfect voice. Or the loudest voice. Or the best tone in the world. But I couldn't stop listening. When he sang, I felt completely and totally engaged. I was hanging on every word. *There* was the mystery ingredient absent in Mr. Dimple.

So, what ever happened to Joe Bob Dimple? I think he's somewhere back home in Fresno growing raisins now. But the other singer? He went on to sell more records than any recording artist of the entire past century. It was Garth Brooks.

The Mystery Ingredient

Ever wonder what makes you want to buy a record album? Or go to a concert? Or search the radio for a certain singer? A great singer seduces your ear and makes you want to spend money on CDs and concert tickets so that you can hear them again and again. What is the mystery ingredient that helped make the difference in the career paths of these two singers? I call it the amazing power of consonants.

Now, you might say, Huh?! That's not exactly what I was expecting. You mean, *consonants*? Those things that aren't a vowel? Whatever *that* is? Yes, more than tone, more than vocal range, more than vibrato, more than volume, what makes a singer stand out from the pack is the way they handle the consonants. Listen to Garth and you'll see why his records sell. He draws us into his singing with bold, in-your-face consonants and the effect is mesmerizing.

Consonants can work for us too when we speak. They grab our listeners' attention and hold on to it. They underscore the intensity of our words and highlight our emotions. Any time you want to *drive* home a point, *implant* a thought, or *punch* up an idea, you can do it with a consonant. Once you know how to use them, you'll be amazed by how radically they increase the expressiveness, clarity, impact, and, ultimately, reception of your words. In fact, I don't know why it is so expensive to buy a vowel on *Wheel of Fortune*. Why buy a vowel when the consonants are worth so much more? Forget about vowels; start *investing* in consonants. Humorist Ruth Ollins had the right idea, "Dwn wth vwls."

Consonants in Action

Let's talk about the way vowels and consonants work together. Vowels are **A, E, I, O, U,** and sometimes **Y** and **W**. Which means that consonants are everything else: **B, C, D, F, G, H, J, K, L, M, N, P, Q, R, S, T, V, X, Z,** and sometimes **Y** and **W**.

In normal conversation, when we want to make a word or an idea stand out, we don't necessarily make that word *LOUDER*. Instead, we **lll-engthen** the consonant at the beginning of the word or syllable we want to emphasize. We create the **illl-usion** of louder by bringing everything to a halt while we wait for that word.

Think about that enduring television cartoon spokestiger Tony the Tiger when he says, "They're **GRRRRRR-eat!**" That long **R** holds us in suspense, drawing us in, making us believe Frosted Flakes might actually *be* great. Now what if he had said it this way? "They're **grEEEAAAt!**" Try it. You see? Not quite the same thing, is it?

If we **rrr-eally** want to emphasize something, we can stretch the consonant a long, **lll-ong** time. Try it yourself. Read that last sentence aloud, lingering on the two marked consonants. "If we **rrr-eally** want to emphasize something, we can stretch the consonant a long, **lll-ong** time." Pretty amazing, huh?

But why does this work? It's because speaking is like music. You have to think of words in speech as a *kind* of music. There is a flow to speech. A natural rhythm. A cadence. If we interrupt or alter that flow, we break the rhythm. This interruption serves to highlight important words.

When you want to draw attention to a particular word, stretch out the beginning consonant and delay the rest of the word. It's a heads up to your listeners that a word you hope they'll pay attention to is about to arrive. Like waiting for the other shoe to drop, it totally arrests your listener and **mmm-akes** them listen.

Consider the great singers of our time. I'll bet when you listen with new ears you'll find that your favorites make good use of consonants. Frank Sinatra was one of the best. He always went straight to the message: "Start **sprrr-eadin'** th' **nnn-ews**." He didn't sing *spreadin'* and *news* louder. Rather, he brought our attention to those words by lengthening the consonants. What if he had sung, "**Staaart spreeeaaad-iiing thuuuh nooows**?" Pretty boring.

Country music giant Patsy Cline was a truly awesome consonant singer. Listen to "Sweet Dreams." She sings, "**Swww-eet drrr-eams** of **eee-you**." Barbra Streisand has made an entire career out of singing on the consonants, as did Maria Callas in opera.

In rock and roll, Bob Seger is a good example. It's downright stirring when he sings his classic, "It's that old time **rrr-ock** 'n' **rrr-oll**." Now what if he had sung it this way, "It's that old time

raaawck and **rooohll**?" You see? It's boring. I tell you, the amazing power of consonants plays a big part in giving these singers their signature sound.

The Temple of Great Vowels

I never learned a great deal about consonants as a conservatory student. You see, most formal singing techniques are vowel-driven. It's as if you are supposed to worship at "The Temple of Great Vowels, No Spitting." My teachers taught me to: "Sing on the vowels, dear, and just try to get through those pesky consonants so you can open up 'The Voice' on the next vowel." Well, I'm sorry, that is not the way *real* people communicate with each other. I didn't learn about consonant power in music school—it took rock and roll to open my eyes.

One day, I was walking past the television set, back when MTV was first being launched. And there was Jefferson Starship wailing away: "We built this city on **Rrr-ock** and **Rrr-oll**." Lead singer Mickey Thomas was doing these wonderfully sustained **R**s and I had one of those life-defining moments—you know, when the lightning flash comes right through your forehead? Suddenly, it was all clear and I said, "Whoa! So, that's what it's been all along? You mean, I've been struggling with vowels when it's really the *consonants* that are important?"

It's easy to become caught up in technique and forget to sound *real*. If it required perfect vowels and a perfect tone, Willie Nelson would never have had a career. He doesn't have a big voice, but he's a wonderful, wonderful singer because he *communicates* when he sings. He talks to us heart-to-heart. That is what people truly value. And that is precisely what the consonants are all about.

Consonants for Clarity and Emphasis

Consonants help us communicate what we really *mean* when we speak. Let me show you how this works. I'm going to give you a four-word phrase: "We still love you." Notice, I've deliberately chosen words containing **Y** and **W**. I'm going to ask you to say this phrase aloud four times in four different ways.

For the first time, I want you to lengthen the **W**, which starts the word *We*. Make a separate **oo** sound for **W**. Imagine that you are a parent talking to your rebellious teenager. "Now all your friends might be mad at you, but we're your parents and **oo-We** still love you."

If you want to give a different emphasis to the same phrase, the next time you say it linger on the **S** of *still*. "No matter how late you've been, no matter how worried we were, we **Ssst-ill** love you." We're using the same four words, but this time it means something a little different.

Then try lengthening the **L** in *love*. "No, you're wrong. We don't hate you, we still **Lll-ove** you." And last, try lengthening the **Y** at the start of *you* with an **ee** sound. "We're not worried about those other kids. Let them stay out late, but we're your parents and we still love **ee-You**."

Go back and listen to how each of these examples puts a different spin on the meaning of those four words. Without a sense of where the emphasis lies, we may imagine something different from the original intention. Take the phrase, "I like cats more than most people." Does this mean that your fondness for cats is greater than the fondness most people have for cats? Or does it mean that given a choice between cats and people, you prefer the company of cats? Changing the emphasis changes the meaning. It's easy to understand why a politician would be nervous about being quoted in print.

The Rhythm of Speech

Say we want to emphasize the word *me* in the sentence "This is important to **ME**." And remembering that speech has a natural cadence that is similar to music, let's emphasize the word *me* by putting it on a strong beat. Like a waltz, it's da-da-dum, da-da-dum, **me**. This is important to **me**. And **me** falls solidly on the last beat.

We're taught in English class that the word *me* has only one syllable. In reality, however, the word *me* has two separate and sequential syllable sounds. First, we articulate the **M** and then the **E**. **M · E**. It's not one sound but two.

Now, the beat can only be at one point. But the word *me* has both an **M** and an **E**. Which of these two letters belongs on the point of the beat? The **M** or the **E**? If you guessed **E**, you were right. In our cadence of speech, we must place the vowel right on the beat. But, if the **E** goes on the beat, where does the **M** fit in? It must go ahead of the **E**, in the space *before* the beat.

And we can start the consonant a little before the beat or a **lll-ot** before the beat. If you want to stress that something is personally important to you, then start the **M** a **lll-ong** time ahead of the beat. You are indicating, "This might not mean much to *you*, but this is really important to **MMM-e**."

But did you notice that when you hold the **M** longer, it is a bit more difficult to make everything fit? There is a limited amount of time in a naturally rhythmic phrase. We can't keep putting stuff *into* the pot without taking something *out* of the pot. How do we find more space for that **M**? We eliminate something. We take time away from the previous word. We shorten the word *to*, or eliminate it, and go directly to the **M**. This is **important t'MMM-ee**. The word *to* will never be missed.

The Filler Words

All words are not created equal. You don't actually *have* to say all of the words merely because they are there. When we speak, we · do · not · pro · nounce · each · and · ev · er · y · syl · la · ble.

People tend to speed-listen in much the same way as they speed-read. When you read a good book, you · do · not · read · from · word · to · word · at · the · same · pace. No, your mind goes from *important* word to *important* word, glossing over nonessential or "filler" words, such as *the, and, that, would, if,* and *but.* Knowing where the sentence is headed, you automatically fill those in based on what your brain expects them to be. If your teenager comes home with a long rambling story that goes on and on for fifteen minutes, all you might hear is "car . . . crash . . . tree."

Filler words are part of the grammar of our language and we need them so that we don't sound like we just stepped out of a cave. But they're sort of the broth in the alphabet soup. We don't really want them to stand out. The listener wants to immediately get to the heart of what we're saying, understand it, digest it, and move on. People would feel inclined to strangle us if we talked like this: "Excuse · me · I · do · not · mean · to · trouble · you · but · I · believe · your · hair · is · on · fire."

Remember: Your listeners are actually speed-listening—skipping from key word to key word, mentally filling in the blanks. So back off everything they supply themselves—*the, and, that, would, if,* or *but*—and you'll have a naturally easy flow to your words. Writer Elmore Leonard put it this way, "I try to leave out the parts that people skip."

The $$ Words

That is how we handle the throwaway words, the filler words. However, certain key words and thoughts *need* time to resonate. So, lengthen the consonants at the beginning of words that are important to your message—the so-called money words. What *are* the money words? They are the one, two, or three words in each phrase that absolutely reduce it down to its basic meaning. They telegraph the essence of what you are saying. If you were leaving a message in the sand on a desert island, you wouldn't write,

> "Help! Our ship sank and we've been here for three days with no water and only coconuts and I don't like coconut, well, once in awhile I'll eat a Mounds bar, but I really prefer Snickers and my lips are chapped and I don't have my Blistex."

"Help" would probably suffice.

In our example about the person with their hair on fire, the money word would surely be *fire*. "Your hair is on **FFF-IRE!**" Listen to how advertising copy on radio and television is always read with consonant emphasis on the money words—punching up the benefits of the product or service, downplaying filler words that might distract from the selling points.

Get the Point?

We've talked about consonants at the beginning of the word. What about consonants at the *end* of the word? What happens when you emphasize them, too? You get double the impact. It's like putting an exclamation point at the end of the word, asking your listener to take special note of what you have just said. Use it when you really want something to sink in.

For example, in a sales meeting, the directive might be: "Sales must be up next quarter." That is the point you want to drive home. Yes, you can emphasize the word *must* by lengthening the **M.** But *must* takes on even more importance when you spend time on both the **M** and the **ST,** sending up an attention alert before and after. "Sales **mmm-u-sssttt** be up next quarter." I think they'll start to get the point.

Repetition + Variety = Memorability

A presentation may be well prepared and full of important information, but attention spans are short. Face it. We are, first and foremost, interested in ourselves and how what someone else is saying relates to *us*. To keep people involved, you have to keep them guessing, "What does this mean for me?"

Suppose you have an important recurring point or theme. In our chat with the account executives, for example, we already know you want them to walk away with the phrase "Sales must be up" tattooed on their brains. Hold their interest in that issue by lengthening different consonants, giving them different ways to think about it.

Every time you bring it up, make it mean something new. "**Sss-ales** must be up next quarter." Or "Sales must *bbbe* up next quarter." Or "Sales must be up **nnn-ext** quarter." Use repetition plus variety. Keep coming back to your main idea, but vary the emphasis each time, and your point will be difficult to miss.

In a song, it is appropriately called a *hook*—that phrase that you can't get out of your head. Ever have that happen? You just can't get a line from a song out of your mind? In Germany, they call it an ear worm. It gets in your ear and you can't get rid of it. Like the hook in a song, you can hook your listener by driving home the same point in different ways.

The Huey Lewis Consonant System

Let's go over some of the main consonant groups and use their individual sounds to create accent and emphasis. Phoneticians, who study the branch of linguistics that deals with the production of speech sounds, recognize twenty or more different categories of consonants and subgroups. I've simplified it to only a few. Of course, sometimes it takes a shoehorn to get them to fit into their categories, but these will get you through what you need to know.

I got a great reaction the day I described these categories to singer Huey Lewis. In fact, he loved the entire concept. He was a great student. He went back to his hotel room and wrote down notes after listening to the tape we made of his session. I guess this is why he's Huey Lewis—he does his homework. He organized what I had told him and brought it back to me the next day written down neatly on three cocktail napkins. *(Why is it that some of our best ideas start out on napkins? Has anybody ever thought of cocktail napkin Post-its!?)* I said, "Here, let me take this and shape it up a little better. I'll give it back to you the next time I see you." That is how this basic list came about—from a cocktail napkin.

Five Ways to Start a Word

VOICED CONSONANTS: THESE HAVE TONE + PITCH + LENGTH:
M   N   L   V   R   Z   TH (in *that*)

Voiced consonants are the easiest to elongate. Like vowels, they have real tone. They have pitch—you can raise or lower their pitch with your voice. They have length—they can last a long time or a short time. For example, "I would **nnn-ever** do that!"

UNVOICED CONSONANTS: THESE HAVE LENGTH BUT NO TONE + NO PITCH:
S   F   T   H   SH   CH   TH (in *think*)

Unvoiced consonants are also easy to stretch. They have no tone and no pitch, but they do have length. They are also called aspirated consonants because you use air in the sound to extend them. For example, "You're **fff-inally** here!"

STOPPED CONSONANTS: THESE HAVE NO TONE + NO PITCH + NO LENGTH:
D   B   P   G (in *good*)   *C* (in *cook*)

What I call the stopped consonants are the tricky ones. They have no tone, no pitch, and no length. So, if our entire premise is predicated on lengthening the consonants, how can we lengthen something that has no length? We don't want to stutter, "I already **d' d' d' did** that!" Fortunately, there is another way.

First, we need to carve out some space so that we can lengthen *something*, which, in this case, is silence. We start by cutting the previous word short. Put your tongue up to the hard palate ridge right above your front teeth and abruptly stop the last part of the word *already* with your tongue. Get ready to say the **D**. But don't. Hold it there. Extend the silence. Then release the **D** with an explosive "pop." The shorter the first word and the longer the silence, the more emphatic it will sound. Example: "I already **dddid** that!"

WORDS THAT START WITH VOWELS: THESE USE A BREAK + A GLOTTAL STOP: *A E I O U*

What do you do about words that start with a vowel? Handle them almost like the stopped consonants, except here you add a voice break—a little glottal stop. It's like a short catch in your voice. For example, "I want **uh'ohnly** the best!"

SOMETIMES Y AND W: THESE ACT LIKE SEPARATE SYLLABLES: *Y* IS LIKE *EE* (in *feel*); *W* SOUNDS LIKE *OO* (in *fool*)

Y and **W** are actually vowel sounds, but when they appear at the beginning of a word as consonants, we pronounce them as independent syllables.

Y sounds like the vowel **E**: **ee-you; ee-young; ee-your; ee-yesterday**. For example, "I'm surprised to see **ee-you!**"

With a few exceptions like *whole* and *who*, **W** is pronounced like the **oo** in *fool*: **oo-what; oo-when; oo-where; oo-why; oo-which; oo-we; oo-was**. For example, "I don't know **oo-what** to do next!"

Did you notice, incidentally, that the way we pronounce the alphabet letter **W** also describes the sound of the letter? We pronounce it: double-**U**. Two **U**s. And if you write two **U**s together, what do they look like? A double **UU**—or **W**.

Onomatopoeia

Some special words reach deep inside your listeners to play on their subliminal consciousness. It's called *onomatopoeia*, a Greek word meaning "the formation of words by imitating sounds." These words are drawn from, and sound like, the meaning of the word. The word *splash* sounds like a splash. *Knock* is sharp and percussive. *Slap*, *sting*, and *spit* all emphasize the *nature* of what they mean in the way they are pronounced. *Mist* is a kind of misty word. *Shine* seems to shimmer and glow. *Glitch* sounds like a glitch to me. The word *cling* sort of holds onto and *clings* to you. The word **rrr-ound** sounds circular.

If you say, "Put your arms **arrrr-ound** me, honey," you can almost *feel* the embracing quality of that word. You feel the roundness. If you play up the qualities of onomatopoeia, you can go beyond intellectual perception into a more visceral response that really hooks people.

Consonants Are the Secret Sauce

Remember, consonants are a powerful tool. Whenever you lengthen a consonant, you **oo-will** get an accent. So be certain that you want one there. Naturally, you will need to experiment and practice to get the knack of it. Use a tape recorder or your outgoing message on your answering machine to record yourself. When you listen back, I think you're going to be shocked by how drastically consonants can manipulate the meaning of what you say.

You will come to see that the richness of our language lies **nnn-ot** in the vowels, but in the consonants. It's like pasta. Vowels are like the noodles—all substance and no flavor. Blindfolded, I don't think I could tell the difference between two brands of plain pasta noodles, but I can definitely taste the difference between tomato sauce and a pesto or alfredo sauce. Consonants are like the sauce. They are full of flavor and spice. They give our speech color, variety, emphasis, intent, and emotion.

Use them boldly and they will make everything you say more effective, dynamic, and motivating. I love what George M. Cohan said to Spencer Tracy, "Whatever you do, kid, always serve it with a little dressing."

Silence Is Golden

CHAPTER FIVE

I WANT to talk about silence. Yes, that's right. Silence.

What, you might ask, does silence have to do with speaking? Surprisingly, much more than you might think. In fact, the space you put *between* your thoughts can be as powerful as the thoughts themselves. Silence does speak a thousand words.

Consider Paul Harvey, a world-renowned radio commentator since 1951. How has he been able to keep his audience riveted to his radio broadcast for so many years? Yes, he has a great voice, but his real genius lies in his ability to hold our attention by creating powerful silences. Paul Harvey is the all-time master of the art of the "power pause." He gets us to listen to what is coming next by making us wait for it.

A lesser speaker might run on and try to get as many words as possible into a short amount of time. It's too much to digest so the mind boggles and turns away. But not Paul Harvey. He sets you up. // He makes you wait. // He draws you in. // And before you know it, he's got your total attention. You *want* to buy anything that he's selling. He seduces your ear with *silence*, and soon you find that you actually *do* want to hear "The **rrr-essst** // of the story."

The Power Pause

What I call a "power pause" is an extension of the long consonant idea. What is the difference? Long consonants work by interrupting the rhythmic flow *within* a phrase, whereas a power pause is a rhythmic pause *between* phrases. Both set up suspense. Both are powerful attention-grabbers.

When do we use the power pause? We use it when we want to give our listeners time to think. This is especially important when we are about to say something that they're not expecting to hear on autopilot.

Andofcourseinthenewmillenniumtheimportanceof cyberspacefishcannotbeunderstated.

What? What was that? You probably didn't catch it. Something about some kind of fish. If I want to talk to you about cyberspace fish right out of the blue, I must give you plenty of time to digest that unusual word combination. You're probably not expecting to hear me say "cyberspace fish." To help those words sink in, I use a power pause both before and after to separate and clarify the words—like this:

And of course, in the new millennium, the importance
of // cyberspace // fish // can not be understated.

A pause *before* the word gets your listeners' attention and pre-
pares them for an unexpected idea. A pause *after* the word gives the
idea time to sink in. If you just forge ahead, your listeners can't
keep up. They either move on with you, failing to grasp what you've
just said, or they stop to digest your bombshell and miss what you
say next. Something important gets lost.

A power pause can also be used to emphasize powerful emotions.
For example, if I say, "That darn dog," you might think the dog
hadn't been very bad. But if I separate those words with abrupt
clipped silence, "That! // Darn! // Dog!," you get the impression
he might have chewed up a favorite pair of Gucci loafers *and* the
new couch.

The Power Pause Hall of Fame

Former British Prime Minister Winston Churchill was a powerful
speaker. His oratory is credited with inspiring in his fellow citizens
the will to survive and fight on during their darkest hours of World
War II. "This is not the end. // It is not even the beginning of the
end. // But it is, // perhaps, // the end // of the beginning."

Comedians make good use of the pregnant pause. Pay attention
to how your favorite funny person manipulates silence. It's not only
the words that make us laugh. The next time you are watching
reruns, listen to how comic characters like Ralph Kramden, George
and Kramer, or Lucy and Ethel set us up for the punch line. Henny
Youngman, the king of the one-liners, knew how to make the most
of a good silence: "Take my wife // please."

There is a brilliant use of silence in the unmistakably droll
humor of Mae West: "I used to be Snow White // but I drifted."
And if a teenager really wanted to play a cruel joke on her parents,

she could say, "Mom, Dad, I'm going to have a baby // sitting job tonight so I won't be home for dinner." It might not seem too funny to her parents, but maybe that is why it's called a "pregnant" pause?

On the other hand, have you noticed how things speed up during the disclaimer segment of car commercials, or when pharmaceutical advertisements rattle on about how the fabulous drug they've just described could cause nausea, dementia, and hair loss? Advertisers don't want you to focus on that. There are few power pauses around the information people *don't* want you to remember. They just zip that stuff right by you.

> Pricedoesnotincludedealerprepcharges,taxes,title,or steeringwheel. Thisdiscountnotavailabletoyou, membersofyourimmediatefamily,oranyoneyouwill everknow.

But just as these run-on words give you no time to digest what is being said, pausing *too long* may make your audience wonder whether you've gone to sleep with your eyes open. It's all in the timing. Mark Twain once remarked, "The right word may be effective, but no word was ever as effective as a rightly timed pause."

Silence in Any Language

Contrary to what most of us in the United States think, English is not the only language spoken on the planet. It is the second or third language for many of our friends and business associates. The world has truly become an international social and business community and we no longer relate only to our neighbors or to those in our own country, but to people all around the world. A gracious use of silence can help you communicate better.

Those who are new to our language need time to translate. Indicate that you respect their struggle to understand by giving them ample opportunity to sort out what you say, making certain they grasp each meaning before you move on. Don't merely repeat the same thing over and over again in a progressively louder voice. Volume is not the problem. Pause before and after the most important units of thought to give people the opportunity to comprehend their meaning.

Keep it simple. Skip the extra verbiage and stick to short, basic phrases. Avoid slang and "five-dollar" words. Take time to ask for confirmation that you are, indeed, being understood and find alternative ways of saying things when your listener seems confused.

Silence—The Negotiation Power Tool

As the world becomes increasingly interconnected, we must learn to negotiate effectively with international business partners of different languages and customs. Every society has its own view of what constitutes too much talking. I'm reminded of the often-told story of the monk who took a vow of silence.

> A monk took a vow of silence when he joined the monastery. He was only allowed to speak two words every ten years. At the end of the first ten years, he said, "Bed hard." At the end of twenty years, he said, "Food bad." At the end of thirty years he said, "I quit." The head monk says, "I'm not surprised. You've done nothing but complain since you got here."

People in the United States tend to be a rather outgoing and verbal bunch who seem to find silence disconcerting. Because it makes *us* uncomfortable, we assume responsibility for *everyone's* comfort and rush in to fill up the void, even if it is only with an annoying "um"—that nervous sound we use to bridge a pesky silence. It is better to say nothing at all than to blurt out the first thing that comes to mind or flail around on "um." We must become comfortable with silence if we want to compete successfully.

Negotiation is like a high-stakes card game. If you want to win, there are certain things you must never do: You certainly don't show your cards to the other side; you don't register your satisfaction with the draw and the way your hand is building; and you don't play your most valuable cards until the right moment. You keep a few aces up your sleeve and hope your opponents reveal their strategies, strengths, and weaknesses without discovering yours. The more you say or reveal to the other side, the weaker your position becomes. Anything you say *can* be used against you.

Negotiators from Asian societies have long known that an effective tactic is making your opponent wait for an answer. When we don't know what other people are thinking, we may become caught up anticipating their strategy and falter in our own. Don't let silence in negotiation throw you. Start thinking like your Asian business partners who consider that "the best way to save face is to keep the lower half of it closed." In business negotiations, as in everyday life, that is often true. Begin to use the power of silence in your negotiations. It's not your job to fill up every silence just because it's there.

Silence Is Power

Silence plays a big role in the way other people perceive us. Who gets more respect? The strong, silent type or the chatty type? How often do you hear, "Mmmmm, he was the strong, *chatty* type?"

Think of the strong silent characters actor Clint Eastwood has played. In those early spaghetti westerns, it seemed as if it took him two days to answer a question. But that gave him an aura of mystery and suspense. It was such a relief when he finally spoke, you just knew it had to be important. He claims the best advice he got from his acting coach was, "Don't just *do* something. Stand there!"

Screen legend John Wayne used to say his entire acting technique rested on one simple trick: He counted silently to three before every line of dialog. On screen, it looked like he was weighing every thought and carefully considering every response. He was probably only saying to himself, "one Mississippi, two Mississippi, three Mississippi," but *I* fell for it every time. And if it worked for the "Duke," think of what it can do for the rest of us.

When you jump right in after someone else has spoken, it appears as if you haven't really been listening or that you don't think what the other person is saying is as important as your response. But if you wait a few beats, it conveys the impression that you're thinking about what they've said and weighing your answer carefully. And in fact, it will *give* you time to prepare a response. Not a bad idea either. The *appearance* of thinking buys you a few seconds to think.

Try the Duke's method of counting to three—silently, of course—to signal that you're digesting and considering every word. No one has to know you're counting, "One, two, three." Don't panic if it feels more like three years than three seconds. You'll get used to it.

You may say, "But I'm the chatty type." And for some of the time that might be acceptable for you. But the trait of being chatty is not very powerful, nor usually very successful. There will be times when you need to "put a sock in it" and hold back from your natural chatty self. When you want to be taken seriously, and your first response is to forge ahead with chatter, stop and use silence to help you stay in control. Count to three.

You Have the Right to Remain Silent

The art of creative silence takes practice. You might be in agreement that "less is more," but sometimes it can take great resolve to do nothing. You must practice using power pauses for impact and clarity when you speak. And it takes practice to learn how to exercise restraint in your exchanges with others.

Listen carefully to speakers whom you find especially effective and engrossing. Pay close attention to the flow of their words. Do you hear a run-on stream of words and sentences? Or do these speakers know how to make good use of a power pause?

Practice using power pauses by reading something aloud, perhaps a passage from a speech, a sales pitch, a book, or a letter to the editor of your local newspaper. Insert pauses before and after key thoughts and money words—wherever you think a good pause will emphasize or clarify what you are saying. Record yourself reading the passage. Listen back to see whether your pauses were effective and your message clear.

Find a willing friend and stage a mock conversation. As you converse, experiment with power pauses. Monitor your partner's body movements. Does your partner hold still and hang on to every word, or did a foot start to swing or a hip shift in place? When they start wiggling around, you've lost them. Record and review these conversations so that you can hear why.

Movie mogul Sam Goldwyn once complained, "I'm exhausted from not talking." It's well worth the effort, however, and will pay off if you work at it. You'll gain new respect for the power of silence when you see how it impacts what you actually do say. Sometimes, especially during a negotiation, silence is a wiser course than saying anything at all. Get used to using the power of silence when you're not under pressure so that you will be accustomed to using it when you do need it. Don't let silence make you uneasy. Welcome silence. Embrace it. Make it your ally.

There is an old Swiss saying that goes like this: *Sprechen ist silbern, Schweigen ist golden* ("Speech is silver, silence is golden."). And the power pause is pure platinum!

CHAPTER SIX

Theme and Variations

NOW HERE is a deep philosophical question for you: What is art? It is one of those questions film and art school students love to ponder. But really, what is it that distinguishes art from the rest of life, the dramatic from the ordinary, a masterpiece from the merely decorative? What makes something *interesting*?

Suppose, in one hand, we have a snapshot of a pretty rose. In the other, we have a picture of a rose painted by Salvador Dali. What makes the Dali painting a work of art and the other simply a pretty picture of a rose?

Or compare a travel video from the state of Colorado to the movie *City Slickers*. One of these is informative and would help us to plan a vacation. But why does the other keep us glued to the screen for two hours, following its crazy adventures all over the state of Colorado?

The question "What is art?" will not be settled in our lifetime. However, it is generally considered that art requires two elements—*conflict* and *resolution*—working hand-in-hand to elevate the ordinary to the extraordinary. Tension and release. Push and then pull.

That's what almost everything in life is about: conflict and resolution. It makes a story interesting. Boy meets girl. Boy loses girl. Boy gets girl. Uh, oh, he loses her again. Does he get her back? Conflict and resolution. Tension and release.

In *City Slickers*, a bunch of wacky guys go out West and they get into scrapes, and they get out of scrapes, and then they get into some more scrapes. We see footage of beautiful Colorado real estate, but what holds our attention is the conflict and resolution.

It works the same way in the visual arts. Maybe the Salvador Dali rose has been pierced through the heart by a bloody thorn. The juxtaposition of an elegant rose and a bloody thorn presents us with a disturbing moment of conflict and the opportunity to resolve it in our own, quite individual, minds. This is art. It captures the imagination and sets it in motion.

Music is especially manipulative, relying on inner conflict for its power. There is always a push-pull. Harmonically and rhythmically, a good piece of music is written to put us on edge, or not, whenever it chooses. Tension builds to a climax of release. And then starts to build again. Over and over. We hate it and we love it. We're suckers for it. But without all this conflict and resolution, things would be pretty dull.

Variety Is the Spice

Variations in our speech patterns provide the conflict and resolution that make what we say interesting and effective. Ever notice how two people can say the same thing and get a completely different reaction? Words only convey the content, however; it is the way we *deliver* our words that signals the emotions behind the content and the kind of response we expect.

It's like that old prison joke. The convicts have been there so long and the jokes are so old that at mealtimes they just call them out by number and everybody laughs. When the new guy tries it and calls out a number, there is dead silence—nobody laughs. Obviously, *he* can't tell a joke. It's not always *what* you say, but *how* you say it, that counts.

Our goal is to make people listen, keep them listening, and motivate them to action. Although it is not necessary to shout to cut through the clutter, the delivery of our words must create impact. And to create an impact, we need a few good techniques for spicing things up when we want to be heard in an information-saturated world. A strong communicator uses a variety of tools that go beyond merely possessing a good voice.

Indeed, variety is the key to speaking effectively. "A foolish consistency is the hobgoblin of little minds," warned Ralph Waldo Emerson. Contrast and surprise provide the push-pull of tension that gets our attention. Remember, tension is not always a pejorative word. Yes, we must avoid tension when we produce a speaking tone, but we should welcome tension/release for its powerful effect on the delivery of our words. Without it, our words may be ignored.

In Chapter 4 and Chapter 5, I showed you how to use the amazing power of consonants and how to manipulate silence. But these are not the only tools available. We can adjust the volume to speak louder or softer. By altering the pitch of our voice, we can speak higher or lower. We can change our color and tone to sound harsh or warm or anywhere in between. We can vary the rhythm and change the tempo to speak faster or slower. We can shout or whisper.

Like singing, speaking is made up of rhythm, melody, and words. Ultimately, your personal style comes down to phrasing—to the way all these elements combine. Both the sound of your voice and the way you deliver your words are instrumental in creating variety and surprise. And you, like any singer, should not be afraid to pull a few surprises and deliver things up with a punch. Duke Ellington, the lengendary jazz musician, was right, "It don't mean a thing if it ain't got that swing."

In this chapter, we will build on everything we have learned thus far to discover how the various elements work together to make what we say more compelling, dynamic, and meaningful. Have you ever found yourself making one of the following complaints:

* No one pays attention to me.

* Other people interrupt me frequently.

* People often finish my sentences for me.

* People don't remember what I've said.

* It seems hard to get anybody motivated.

That is about to change.

Try practicing everything in a slightly exaggerated manner at first to speed up the learning process. Once you have mastered the technique, you can tone it down to normal. Use your tape recorder for a reality check when you think you might be going too far.

Crank Up the Volume

Let's look at something we can fix simply by adjusting the volume. How about that most common of complaints that nobody seems to pay attention? Well, try turning *up* the volume. Maybe your signal is weak. Maybe it is such an effort to reach out and tune you in that people merely tune you out. If people can't hear you, it's frustrating for everyone.

To see where your voice stands on the volume scale, find a few friends willing to let you record your conversations with them. How loud are you compared with your friends? Is your volume set on 2 or 10? Are you getting through? A weak voice may be perceived as a sign of personal weakness, whereas a strong voice exudes power, authority, and confidence.

When you want to turn up the volume, go back to what you learned about breathing, support, and resonance. Gather your support under you and resonate in your teeth so that your voice can project. Remember passive breathing and be sure to tuck under. And stay out of your throat. If we keep our technique fresh, it will be there when we need it. With greater volume, there is greater need.

But all things in moderation. Unrelenting volume invades the aura of protective space other people establish around themselves. They resent having to defend their boundaries and feel cornered if you assault them too long. The term "loud and obnoxious" springs to mind. Invade at your own risk. It's best to save being loud for when you really mean it.

Vary the Volume

Alternating the volume of your voice punches up individual words and phrases. Being loud startles people into attention. When the situation requires, like when the cat's in danger of being blenderized, you may need to yell. But shouting doesn't work well for long. See what using tension and release does instead. Lower your volume suddenly and it suggests something different is about to happen. This attention-grabbing effect is similar to a power pause. It draws us in and sets us up for the next important point.

Speaking in a very quiet voice has been known to have its own special inverse power and can be very engaging when used by certain people. It worked well for Jacqueline Kennedy, Alfred Hitchcock, and Mr. Rogers. But it's risky. Only a very confident person has the courage to speak at a volume that demands that others draw in to listen. "True strength is delicate," sculptor Louise Nevelson once observed.

Strike a happy balance. If you are too soft, you might sound wimpy. If you are too loud, you could scare little children. Try using conflict and resolution, push-pull, tension and release.

Like a great singer, a skilled communicator knows how to build. Dropping off before you finish will rob your voice of conviction. We've all known people who start each sentence with a flourish, but drop off into some inaudible abyss by the end, thereby draining their words of forward momentum. The energy deflates and must be regenerated with each new start. It's exhausting. Plus, we're probably missing important information there at the end.

Here's the Pitch

Changes in pitch can work well for us, too. *Webster's Dictionary* defines pitch as "the difference in the relative vibration frequency of the human voice that contributes to the total meaning of speech." In other words, pitch is an important contributor.

Have you ever wondered why advertisers choose a preponderance of male voices to speak for their products when women make more purchases? A low voice is generally perceived as belonging to someone in a position of authority. When a woman's voice is used in advertising, the speaker usually has the low rich voice of a Lauren Bacall or Kathleen Turner. A high voice signals youth and inexperience, implying this is someone who could be easily disregarded. We don't hear a voice like comedian Lucille Ball's on many commercials.

When you want your speaking voice to convey wisdom and authority, lower your pitch. But stay within the limits of your natural range. If you're starting out like Lucille Ball, don't try to become

Barry White. Use lots of support to keep your body resonant and make sure your head and chest are free to vibrate. If you're lowering the pitch, it is important to have a loose jaw. Don't let it tighten.

You can punch up important words by using pitch as well as volume. At crucial moments, when you want to exude energy and excitement, raise the pitch of your voice. It can be a powerful motivator. Remember, a higher pitch needs extra support or it will sound shrill. A high pitch can put people on edge or it can motivate them. A low pitch can soothe or bore.

The Rise and Fall

And did you know that you can pause at any point and still keep your audience at full attention? Slight alterations in pitch, signaling that you intend to continue, hold the listener through a pregnant pause.

First, let your voice rise on the last word *before* the pause to create a feeling of suspense. Pause. Then, start the word *after* the pause on the same high note. Raising the pitch before the pause keeps the audience suspended *during* the pause. If you let the pitch drop, it sounds like you've finished.

A rise in pitch also indicates the difference between a sentence and a question. Lifting your voice at the end signals that you are expecting a response, thereby inviting the listener to take the next step. Be careful, though, it can be dangerous. You may fall into the Valley Girl Syndrome—an especially tiresome habit of lifting at the end of every sentence. There are only a limited number of times that your listener wants to be prompted by what seems to be a question, but isn't.

Anatomy of a Whine

On the other hand, a drop in pitch defines that most painful of human sounds—the dreaded whine. If you're tired of your friends and want to improve your whining skills, you are in the right section.

Whining is a two-note descending voice slide. The interesting thing about whining is that it tends to follow a fixed pattern of notes. In a random, completely unscientific test of whiners, I found that they consistently slid between two notes by using a particular interval that in music is called a diminished fifth, or augmented fourth.

Intervals indicate the number of steps between two notes. A true whine slides down seven half-steps. Any other arrangement of notes just doesn't produce a good, convincing whine.

In medieval times, this interval was deemed so offensive to the ear that it earned the name *Diabolus in Musica*, the "Devil in Music," and was avoided religiously by early church music composers. Not much has changed in the way we feel about it today.

What makes whining so annoying (in addition to its nasal quality) is that its dissonant arrangement of notes never resolves in harmony. It breaks the rules of conflict and resolution. And the longer the pattern continues, the more desperate we become to escape. Like the shower scene music in Alfred Hitchcock's *Psycho*, it really puts us on edge.

Multiple Personalities

Fine shadings in voice color convey dramatically different attitudes. We have the capacity to manipulate our timbre, or tone of voice, to make it soothing, calming, urgent, persuasive, suspenseful, wise, commanding, or motivating. We take on different voices for different situations and for the many roles we play. However, it's more like the *Twenty Voices of Bob* than the *Three Faces of Eve*. Each of these voices speaks for us at one time or another and they are all at our disposal whenever we need them.

Warm, round tones are soothing and calming. My grandmother used to say, "You catch more flies with honey than you do with vinegar." And you get this honeyed warmth by relying on support to help produce a tone that is tension-free. Use it to help diffuse a difficult situation or when you want to be persuasive. Bad things don't seem so bad when they are delivered with positive overtones.

On the other hand, don't deliver tragic news in a gleeful tone like the local newscaster I heard one night who used a way-too-brittle and cheerful voice to inform us that "a bus went off a cliff today, killing all 66 passengers, most of them children." This is inappropriate inflection.

A breathy quality can be suggestive. Not many people can get away with using it all the time—Marilyn Monroe being one notable exception. In some situations, a breathy quality can imply urgency. But you'll have to throw in a harsh and grating tone and some serious volume to get the dog's attention when you want him off the couch, *now*.

Whispering can be very effective. Whispering is not quite the same as speaking softly. Changing your tone to a whisper makes what you say more intimate and compelling. I love what Irish sage Patrick Murray had to say: "If you cannot get people to listen to you any other way, tell them it's confidential."

Sometimes you need to sound calm and steady, even when you're not. Taking a moment to center yourself will keep anxiety, anger, or frustration from showing in your voice. Concentrate on passive breathing and low support. Don't simply count to ten, take ten low breaths and use this moment to reaffirm the support muscles you need for steadying your voice.

Want to convince me of something? You're halfway there if I can sense your entire body is involved. Shallow breathing and a lack of support give the impression you don't stand behind what you're saying. Good technique makes you sound committed.

The important thing is to vary the color of your voice to fit the situation. The tone you use reflects how you really feel about what you're saying. And remember—nobody likes a whiner.

The Rhythm Method

When we talk, we set up a cadence that is similar to the beat we hear in music. Words have a natural rhythmic flow, there *is* a kind of beat there, even if it is not as formal as it is in music. And like music, our ears become lulled into expecting that the flow will continue at the same pace. When the pattern is broken and the flow is interrupted, the sudden shock instantly refocuses our attention.

A pause is the most direct way to interrupt the flow. The artist currently known as Prince once told Larry King that he finds, "Space is a sound too, and it can be used very inventively." Pauses separate words into digestible units of information and draw focus to the main points of the message. Whenever you make them wait for something, people always listen more carefully.

Accentuate the Positive

Of course, the other way to interrupt the flow is with long consonants. I urge you to use the consonants, not so you'll have perfectly clipped diction, but because that interruption adds variety and suspense to whatever you say. Don't be afraid to lengthen consonants, but choose carefully and save this technique for the money words. Always remember to lighten up on the filler or throwaway words.

The Pacemaker

Varying the tempo, or speed, of what you say is another way to apply conflict and resolution to the rhythmic pattern. You can go faster or . . . you . . . can . . . go . . . slower. Different tempos are appropriate for different situations. To draw attention to major points—slow down. When you slow things down, you naturally use more silence and longer consonants, which gives those points ample time to resonate.

If you want to set your listeners up for something important, pick up the tempo before you make that point—pause—and then slow down to deliver it. Carry your listeners forward and then make them wait. It's classic tension/release at work.

Each of us tends to fall into our own unique pattern of melody and rhythm when we deliver our words. It's one of the things that defines our individual speaking styles. But listening to someone who *always* uses the same pattern can be mind-numbing. Don't fall into a pattern that could be described as singsong. A steady pattern can lull us to sleep. Vary the length of your phrases to keep the surprises coming. On the other hand, an undeviating irregular pattern can lose its power to grab our attention and can get on our nerves instead.

Monotone

So far we've talked about the possibilities of variety. Where does the lack of variety—a monotone—fit in? Obviously, a monotone is not a good choice for the fundamental color of your voice, but sometimes it can be useful. A monotone has a place in our lexicon of options because it can project an ominous, understated power, adding drama to a situation through sustained tension.

The shark theme in the movie *Jaws* is an excellent example of sustained tension; it ignores the normal rules of conflict/resolution. The theme is built on a dissonant chord and a gradually accelerating beat that take a long time to resolve. The conflict hammers at us relentlessly and doesn't resolve until somebody gets bitten in half. (*If the* Jaws *sequels continue, someday we'll line up to see* Jaws 8—The Gumming.)

If you really want to drive home a message, nothing tops a well-considered monotone. Suppose you're telling your teenager, "No, you can not have the keys to the new Lexus!" These words, when delivered in a monotone, can be quite specific and clear.

Cutting Through the Clutter

We're under assault from the avalanche of words that enter our ears every day. It's hard to escape other people's words while still having some thoughts of our own. So, we learn to tune things out. The amazing thing about our senses is that we have a built-in limiter, and when our systems overload, we can block things out to a certain degree.

Conflict and resolution can help you to penetrate even the deepest fog. In a tuned-out world, you must use variety and surprise to get through and keep things interesting. Each of these variation techniques adds color and interest to what you say, and has significant influence on how people perceive you and react to you.

Now let's get some practice putting these principles into action in the real world. Record yourself responding to the following scenarios:

* You're late for work—again. Call your boss.

* Your teenager wants to drive the new car. Explain the rules.

* You're firing an employee who has become a friend.

* You're dining at an expensive restaurant and have just received your meal. It's smothered in onions and you're allergic. (Substitute *your* phobia.) Send it back.

* Make up your own scenario—why not use this exercise to rehearse a conversation you've been putting off?

Listen to your responses and then answer the following questions:

* Do I emphasize my most important points?
* Does anything important get lost in my delivery?
* Am I clear about what I want?
* Am I convincing?
* What conclusions would someone draw from the way I speak?
* Would I get what I want?

Practice these scenarios until you feel certain you would get the results you desire. You'll soon find that the principles of conflict and resolution will make life a little easier by helping you resolve your conflicts as they arise.

applications

Speeches That Make People Listen

WHAT IS the number one phobia in America? Not the fear of gaining five pounds. Or the fear of a bear market. It's glossophobia, which is the fear of public speaking. The fear of speaking in public ranks even higher than the fear of death in the minds of many people.

Face it, though, we all have to do it sometimes. It may be part of your job, an activity at your church, or raising a toast to a friend. At some time or other, you're going to have to get up and make a presentation. Like any other live performance, public speaking—or even running weekly staff meetings—can be nerve-wracking.

But it doesn't have to be scary and it doesn't have to be a chore. If you prepare well, it can be a breeze—and maybe even an opportunity to be creative and make some music of your own. If you think about it, you'll realize that during a speech you have greater control over your performance than even most singers do. You're the composer of your "song" as well as the artist who performs it. You write the words. You write the melody. You set the rhythm and pace. And you deliver it. It's up to you to write a speech that is interesting; I can't help you there. But I can help you to make it *sound* interesting.

Blueprint for a Speech

Speeches range from a formal (possibly paid) presentation in front of an audience of strangers to the report you give at the annual board meeting. In the following example, let's assume that you're going to be delivering a big-deal formal speech—one you're actually going to write out and learn. In the weeks preceding the big day, you would do the following:

* Write your speech.
* Make decisions about phrasing.
* Construct a phrasing schematic.
* Study the equipment.
* Work on physical presence.
* Neutralize stage fright.
* Rehearse and review.

Speech Under Construction

As you write your speech, think about how to phrase what you're writing and how you want the melody and rhythm to go. Plan out the sentence structure with pacing in mind—long sentences slow down the pace; short sentences pick up the tempo. You can build toward major points by starting off with sentences of normal length that become progressively shorter and punchier. A gradual increase in pitch, volume, and tempo adds to the forward energy, making your point ever more compelling as you build toward the conclusion.

A Quick Schematic

I've developed a marking system that makes it easy to incorporate the devices we've learned. Even if you're not planning to read your speech straight from the page, this schematic will help you practice bringing these elements into play. *(Doesn't "schematic" sound like a Ronco product? "The new Ski-matic! Use it with your Pocket Fisherman.")* Before you print out your completed speech, double-space and enlarge the text for easy reading. Make several copies so that you can try your speech in different ways and take notes.

Begin by reading the entire speech aloud. Determine which information you need to emphasize and which individual words you want to bring out with consonants, volume, pitch, or a change in voice color. Don't just go for the brain; go for the heart, too. Use all the elements of variety and surprise. Record these practice sessions and study them. This is a fluid situation; be ready to change your mind often as you continue to practice and fine-tune. Experiment until you're satisfied with the phrasing and your delivery has become consistent.

Now, start building the schematic by indicating phrase breaks and accents. As you make decisions, mark them in your practice copies. Then transfer these performance notes to your final text. I suggest using forward slashes and an extra space for marking a pause, capitalization for indicating a rise in volume or pitch, and boldface type for signaling a long consonant.

Keep Your Options Open

To illustrate, let's use one of my all-time favorite quotes: "Work is the meat in the hamburger of life." I once saw this quote attributed to McDonald's founder, Ray Kroc, but it was so many years ago that I can no longer verify that the phrase is his. But if he didn't say it, I'll be glad to take the credit. This short phrase has many options. It may be phrased simply this way:

"Work is the meat // in the hamburger of life."

Or I might want you to look at it a little differently. If I want to let something specific sink in, I capitalize that word or phrase to indicate a raise in pitch or volume or both:

"Work is the MEAT // in the hamburger of life."

Should I wish to lengthen consonants for even greater emphasis, I can boldface as well as capitalize. If there is a central theme or key word you're pushing, you'll get results if you drive it home like this many times during your presentation:

"**WORK** // is the meat // in the hamburger of life."

Now let's look at a slightly longer piece. Read both of the following examples aloud, putting emphasis and pauses where they are indicated. It will quickly become apparent that the possibilities are limitless.

Let the WORD go forth from this time and place, // to friend and foe ALIKE, // that the torch HAS been passed // to a new generation of Americans, // **BORN** in this century, // TEMPERED by the war, // **DISCI-PLINED** by a hard and bitter peace, // **PROUD** of our ancient heritage, and UNWILLING // to witness

OR permit // the slow undoing of those human rights // to which this nation has ALWAYS been committed, // and to which we ARE committed today // at HOME // and AROUND the world.

LET the word go forth // from THIS time and place, // to FRIEND // and FOE alike, // that the TORCH has been passed to a NEW generation of Americans, // born in THIS century, // tempered by the WAR, // disciplined by a HARD and BITTER peace, // proud of our ancient HERITAGE, and unwilling to WITNESS // or PERMIT // the slow UNDOING of those human rights to which THIS NATION // has always been COMMITTED, // and to which we are committed TODAY // at home // AND around the world.

—John F. Kennedy, Inaugural Address
January 20, 1961

You see, you have options. After all, as the composer and performer of your speech, you're in charge. You can plot pauses and accents wherever you want to emphasize something. You can direct your listeners' attention to the points you want to make. You can give them new ways to consider the same idea. Take time to write in the phrase and accent markings with the same amount of care that you used to write in every word. Your schematic is the blueprint that will help you organize your speech and bring it to life.

The schematic will even help you to learn your speech. When your phrasing includes melody and rhythm, your words begin to resemble music, helping you to recall entire units of text. It's always easier to remember a song than to remember only words. After all, isn't that how you learned the alphabet? Remember that little childhood ditty? *"A B C D E F G . . .* Now I've learned my *ABCs. . . ."*

Test-Drive the Equipment

Since we've decided that this is a formal speech you're giving, you're going to have a microphone, a sound system, a lectern, and all the trappings of a big-time presentation. The microphone might seem like a good idea at first, but it brings into play that most unreliable of mixed blessings—the sound system. If something can go wrong, it will—and usually does.

Most of the places where we speak are not inclined to be acoustically friendly. You'll be lucky to have any help at all from the natural room acoustics. It would be nice if every meeting room were equipped with state-of-the-art microphones and a great public-address system, but you should be prepared for most of them to be rather limited.

It's a good idea to test-drive the equipment whenever possible. Every room you speak in will be different, so try to get in there before the big day and find out what is waiting for you. Take along a friend to be your "ears" and help you determine the levels and effects.

Introduce yourself to the person in charge of the sound equipment (assuming there *is* one) and pick their brain about the options and quirks of this particular equipment. Ask that someone be on-site during the speech to make adjustments if necessary. Be very, *very* nice to that person. You need them on your side.

Find the right volume level and experiment with whatever sound effects may be available. You might add some reverb (or echo effect) to make your voice sound warm and encompassing, but be careful not to go overboard here. If you set the levels a little "wet" to warm up the sound of your voice, you risk creating the effect of stadium delay. By the time the sound clatters around the room, it can develop enough echo to call in an entire herd of Swiss goats.

At your sound check, be aware that the acoustics of the room will dampen when there are more bodies present to absorb the sound, but at least you can get some feeling for how the equipment and room will respond. Make a written list of all your settings and requests and pass on a copy to the person who is responsible.

During your test-run at the venue, take the extra precaution of asking about the usual temperature setting for the room. One summer day during a heat wave, I failed to plan ahead for air conditioning and wore a favorite silk summer suit to speak in a venue that was so teeth-chatteringly cold that I visibly shivered for the entire miserable hour. As part of your planning, make a note to dress prepared for a change in the indoor weather.

Mic Dancing

If you're not accustomed to using a microphone, it's a good idea to start learning how to use one long before the big day. Your trip to the venue will tell you which type of microphone you'll be using and may give you an opportunity to work with it.

A microphone is either omnidirectional or unidirectional. An omnidirectional microphone picks up signals from the entire surface of the microphone, whereas the unidirectional microphone has one so-called sweet spot that is ideal for speaking. For both types of microphones, it is important to maintain a consistent volume level throughout your speech.

In general, the distance from your lips to the microphone determines two things—volume and presence. Speaking close to the microphone gives your voice warmth and immediate presence. As you move farther away, the sound appears distant and thin. I always recommend getting as close to the microphone as the equipment will allow. The closer you get to the microphone, the warmer and fuller your voice will sound. All rock musicians know this—that's why they seem to swallow the mic.

With a hand-held microphone, you have instant control. Your arm brings it closer to your lips when you want to say something in a whisper or moves it farther away when you're building to a climax and the volume peaks. There is more freedom for moving around because you can take the microphone with you. You can pace. You can move in toward your audience. You can retreat.

One pitfall is that, in the throes of a gesture, your arm may wave the microphone out of range. Make certain that the microphone moves when you move and not on its own. Another problem is that it can be nearly impossible to work from notes because one hand is always busy with the microphone.

Fixed Position

If the microphone is in a fixed position, either on a stand or attached to a lectern, you need to work a little harder to relate to it. Unlike using a hand-held, where both you and the microphone can move around, this type is never going to move.

The trick here is to maintain a consistent distance from the microphone, without feeling like you're trapped in a vise. An omni-directional microphone is less restrictive than one that is unidirec-tional and gives you more latitude for moving around. You want to stay as loose and free as you can. Explore how much lateral range you can use while still keeping your lips the proper distance from the microphone.

Be sure the microphone is not placed too high. Most people set it at lip height and neglect to factor in the slight dip that occurs when they tuck under to support. As a result, they are forced to stretch up to speak, which strains the voice and makes it sound tense. Instead, position the microphone at lip level, and then drop it down about an inch. That should accommodate the drop in height and put your lips right at the sweet spot when you support.

Returning to the Elvis analogy, if you round over the microphone the way he did, you can direct the resonance up to your head for a warm, rich sound. Try the following experiment: Make a long **EEEEEEE** sound. As you're making that sound, first tip your head gently forward, and then angle it back and lift your chin. Hear how the sound becomes warmer and richer as you arch forward and how it strangles off when you pull your head back? Round your head over the microphone, press into the floor with the balls of your feet, use your lower abdominal muscles, and you'll be in the optimal position for speaking. *(This might be another good time to go into one of those Elvis imitations.)*

There is yet another type of microphone that you may encounter. A Lavalier microphone is worn on the body. The transmitter is carried discreetly at the waist and is attached to a tiny microphone that is clipped to a person's collar. It leaves both hands and body free to move and puts no barriers between you and your audience.

A word to the wise, though, if you're a chest thumper, you're in trouble here. Even the most gentle chest thump registers as a loud dull thud. Also, be careful to aim your voice at the microphone. When you turn away, the sound may drop off suddenly as the direction of your head changes. Always be conscious of where the Lavalier is attached and move your entire body when you change direction, not only your head.

Run (and Bark) With the Big Dogs

Long before the big day, you will want to work on your personal presence. What is the first impression your audience has of you? They see you. And the way you carry yourself sets the tone for how they will respond. Presence begins with what I call the position of power:

* Balance on the balls of your feet.

* Tuck under slightly for support.

* Keep your shoulders down.

* Arch up with the back of your neck.

* Keep your chin low.

* Look up from below. (Use your "Elvis eyes.")

This is a universally commanding position that radiates personal power and control. Think of how it translates to the animal kingdom. Have you ever noticed the way two dogs present themselves in a showdown?

When two dogs meet, they posture to establish which one of them is dominant. The stronger dog asserts its dominance by lifting to its fullest height, with head and ears erect. That dog looks down on the weaker dog, which assumes a lower position, seemingly offering up its vulnerable throat to the more dominant dog. They are establishing presence and dominance. It works the same way with people.

Fortunately for us, this ideal position for communicating personal presence is also ideal for engaging support and resonance. Maybe it's no coincidence. If you're using the position of power, you're already halfway there. Now you just have to remember to put it all to work.

During the weeks before your presentation, make sure you practice the vocal exercises. Voice technique is an ongoing process and takes time to become part of you. You can't wait until the big day to think about it. It's not like that time you aced the biology quiz even though you waited until the night before to read the chapter.

It's more like bodybuilding—you don't pump iron around the clock for the last few days before the Mr. Universe competition and win the title.

Coward Control

I saw this graffito on a wall in a recording studio the other day: "Try to relax, or we'll find someone who can." It is a cruel line, because nothing makes a person tighten up faster than telling them to relax. Nobody wants to think they're not relaxed. "Relax? What do you mean, relax? I *am* relaxed!!!"

Stage fright is normal—even useful. It gives our words energy and edge. But when it becomes excessive and counterproductive, we must take steps to neutralize it. Let's see whether we can take some of the fear and loathing out of your presentation by using a little trick I learned from acting coach Jim DeBlaises.

Ask yourself what you're afraid will happen. What is the worst thing you can imagine? Do you think you'll fall down? Your voice will crack? You'll get lost? What are your worst fears? Confront them. Make a list of all the things you think could possibly go wrong. Now do them. If you're afraid that your voice will crack, read your speech and try to make it crack. If you're afraid that you'll forget the words, okay, do that—deliver your speech and forget the words. If you're worried you might stumble over your words, practice stumbling. Make all the mistakes you can think of. Just go crazy. Practice giving a *terrible* speech.

This won't be as easy as it sounds. You will soon discover that it is more difficult to make mistakes than you would think. In fact, it is almost as hard to deliberately make mistakes as it is to deliberately be perfect. But after you've done it a few times, the terror is gone and your fears seem funny. Put some practice time in on this. It's not sufficient merely to know about this technique—you must do it.

Everyone deals with nerves in their own way. Former U.S. President Harry Truman's words, "If you can't stand the heat, get out of the kitchen," come in handy whenever I start losing my nerve. Of course, that's where I want to be—in the kitchen where all the action is! I'm reminded of why I'm doing this in the first place. If that doesn't work for you, there is always the trick comedian Carol Burnett used to keep things in perspective. She recommends you visualize your audience naked, but only if you can do so without snickering.

Hold Rehearsals

Now you're ready to hold rehearsals. Practice your speech in front of a video camera, at first on your own, then in front of friends. Videotape and review everything. Include all elements of your speech from start to finish, not only the words and delivery but gestures and body position, too. Let your body follow the lead your voice takes. Gestures may or may not be part of your repertoire of expression, but if they are, they should start in the heart and move through the voice before they turn up in your hands. Of course, you want to appear relaxed and natural. But be bold. A true star manages to be both real and larger than life simultaneously. This is the time to experiment.

Don't clasp your hands behind your back because you can't think of anything else to do with them. Perfectly normal people, who wouldn't be caught dead running around town with their hands behind their backs, will do just that when faced with a microphone. Suddenly, it's like, "What am I going to do with these things at the end of my arms? Let's stick them behind my back!" Besides looking really dumb, it throws your body alignment off, making it difficult to support.

I discovered how important this is one day when I was in the studio recording a song for the movie *The Good Old Boys*. I was having trouble with a high note that shouldn't have been a problem, when I realized I had fallen into the trap of clasping my hands together behind my back and had completely lost my support. You can't support with your hands behind your back and the natural line of your body off center. Arms and shoulders should remain loose and free.

As you critique the videos of your practice performances, make note of what you want to improve. To gauge your voice and delivery, listen to only the audio portion without the picture. To evaluate the impact and appropriateness of your gestures and stance, try watching with the sound switched off. Add some practice with a microphone if you have access to the equipment.

It's Almost Show Time

So, your speech is written, you've rehearsed with your schematic, you've done your best to stave off an acoustic nightmare, you've worked on your "coward control," and you've fine-tuned your performance. Now you are ready for the final phase of preparation as you pull everything together for the big moment.

Speaking, like singing, is an athletic event. You must schedule accordingly by starting the day before, when you make sure to use your voice as little as possible and to get a good night's sleep. We want your body, brain, and voice to be in peak condition, ready to take center stage.

Because you've stuck to your plan, you are well rested and up in time to do some stretching and light exercise or to take a brisk walk to limber up and get the juices flowing. All of which helps to relieve pre-show tension.

Avoid caffeine in its various forms. Caffeine dries a throat out quickly, and gives us a short-term productivity spurt that declines as the rush wears off. Plus, you don't need anything that will add to the jitters on that day. Let the early morning exercise wake you up instead.

Eat something light at least two hours before the event. No one wants to hear your stomach complaining. Besides, you need the energy. However, you should skip dairy products because they're mucus-producing. The only thing worse than sounding like you need to clear your throat is actually clearing your throat. Drink plenty of water. Anxiety may give you dry mouth.

Physical preparation ties in with mental preparation. While taking your walk, rehearse your speech in your mind and visualize yourself making the speech. Six-time world champion boxer Sugar Ray Leonard once explained that he spent the day of a fight visualizing that night's event. He choreographed the match in his head and played out the entire fight in his mind. Then he just showed up at ringside and ran it the way he wanted it to go. It appears to have worked; he had a long and very successful career. Visualize yourself delivering the speech just the way you want it to go from beginning to end. Focusing on fears only reinforces them.

Take time to warm up your voice. The purpose of a warm-up is not only to limber up the vocal cords but also to reacquaint your body, brain, and voice with the mechanisms you want to bring into play. Start with passive breathing. Do the exercises from Chapter 3 that engage support. Concentrate on finding a good resonant buzz in your voice.

Don't let nervous chatter before the speech or during a break rob your voice of its power, because talking can tire it quickly. Rest your voice and collect your thoughts instead. When you do have to talk, use it as an opportunity to reinforce your technique.

If you find you're last on the schedule to speak and seated at the head table, your warm-up may be a distant memory and your nerves a little frayed. Keep going back to passive breathing to calm and center you, as well as to remind you to breathe that way when you're out in front.

Last Call for Nerve Control

You're moments away from show time. So here are a few final words:

When you're speaking to a group, you have little control over the possible distractions that could sabotage your message. But all these preparations have left you feeling ready and relaxed so that not much can throw you off course. Count on your knowledge of technique to get you out of on-the-spot acoustic problems. When things go wrong, sometimes you have no choice but to plow on.

Don't be surprised if the sound equipment settings have somehow mysteriously changed and you're awash with echo. These things happen. It's up to you to compensate. *Slow down.* Keep your phrases short—leave plenty of time to accommodate the echo. Give your important words and thoughts enough space to settle down and sink in. The audience will be grateful they don't have to struggle to understand you.

Microphone feedback is the electronic equivalent of raking your fingernails across a blackboard, only amplified and much, *much* worse. It is guaranteed to put everybody on edge. If you experience feedback, quickly position yourself farther away from the microphone and use more support to project your voice.

Not all distractions are equipment-related. Acknowledge what is happening around you. If the waiter drops a tray of glasses, incorporate it into your presentation. "No thanks, I'll take one later." The proliferation of cell phones almost guarantees that one will go off at some point. People hear it. Don't be thrown, but find a way to improvise and include it.

I was singing a serious chamber music recital in Berkeley, California, one evening when a large, happy, black retriever wandered in and settled down at my feet onstage, pleased to have found a place where he could be the center of attention. I had little choice but to play to the dog as the love object of the tragic song I was singing at the time. Composer Franz Schubert, no doubt, is still turning in his grave.

But my favorite story of fast-thinking comes from singer Kimber Clayton. She made a big entrance onstage one night, tripped on a step, and skidded all the way across the stage on her chin. As the audience gasped, she brushed it off with a flourish, "And that, ladies and gentlemen, was the talent portion of our program!"

You may not *be* relaxed, but you have to *appear* relaxed. You've already taken steps to neutralize stage fright by realizing your fears and acting them out. Now let passive breathing keep anxiety from taking over your voice. Take ten low relaxed breaths to center yourself.

It's Show Time!

Now that you are here, don't suddenly develop a tone of voice that alienates your audience by talking *at* them. Instead, talk *to* them. A conversational style of speaking brings a human touch to a presentation. My advice? Always speak as if you were talking intimately into the ear of *one* person. Personalize your delivery by focusing on one person at a time, speaking directly to that individual as if to a close friend.

Think about the words. Don't become so caught up in technique that you forget what you're talking about. Remember why you're giving this speech. Carry yourself loosely, but use the position of power. Draw on your lower body for support. Deliver your speech the way you've practiced it. Manipulate the phrasing and use what we've learned about pacing, variety, timing, consonants, and moments of silence. And keep breathing. This is not the time to start holding your breath.

You're ready. There is nothing left to do now but deliver!

Dances With Words

We've just gone through the steps for an upscale speech. Only *you* can decide how important it is that you perform well in this event and how much effort you want to put into preparing for it. When you're off the podium and making your report at a meeting, you can let things relax a bit as circumstances become less formal and more improvisational.

It should always look easy—no one has to know about the hours of careful preparation that went into making it look easy. Technique and preparation give you freedom. If you speak with a voice that is confident and clear, they'll never know you are nervous. In truth, most people would much rather see you succeed than fail. It's your job to take them there.

Speaking in public can be a wonderful experience—creative, rewarding, and exhilarating. Peggy Noonan put it beautifully: "A speech is poetry: cadence, rhythm, imagery, sweep! A speech reminds us that words, like children, have the power to make dance the dullest beanbag of a heart."

Now enjoy the applause. You've earned it.

Turn Up the Sales Volume

"EVERYONE LIVES by selling something," observed author Robert Louis Stevenson, and he was right. Selling is a large part of what you do every day, and will continue to do for the rest of your life. It doesn't matter whether or not you have the word *sales* in your job description or title. Business is all about selling yourself and selling your ideas—even if only at the job interview.

Life itself is about selling. Try to think of a time when you are using your voice and *not* selling. Selling your kids on the idea of brushing their teeth, selling your boss on the idea of a raise, or selling the cat on the idea of coming down out of the tree—it's all still sales.

Sales Duet

The art of making a sales pitch is like singing a duet. Only you don't know yet exactly what the words and music are going to be. You must improvise as you go and take your cues from your duet partner. Your part is to tell the potential customer why they need what you're selling. The customer chimes in with a reason why they don't. You counter with another argument in favor of your product. The customer throws out another objection. Hopefully, you will reach a harmonious conclusion.

If only it were so simple.

If delivering a speech can be equated to a solo performance, the unknowns your partner brings to the table make a sales duet a much more volatile and improvisational situation. You must try to lead your partner through the duet the way you want it to go, but you are not the only one who controls the direction things will take; you must read signals from the other person's voice and be prepared to follow as well.

The Tough Get Going

Sales is a tough business. In spite of your best efforts, you can expect to experience rejection far more frequently than success—it goes with the territory. And it takes a special kind of person to live comfortably with repeated rejection. Don't think about a career in sales if you're in therapy for anger management. One way to be successful—and still retain a grip on your sanity—is to never push a product you wouldn't recommend to your own family. A sales job shouldn't have to mean selling out.

On the other hand, sales can be very lucrative. Self-starters are attracted because, to a large extent, you are the master of your own destiny in sales. The rewards relate more directly and more immediately to the effort than they do in many professions. But things get tougher and more competitive as the rewards increase; I'm sure we'd find a difference in remuneration between selling ice cream cones and selling ice cream companies. And sometimes the rewarding moments can seem few and far between. You owe it to yourself and your employer to take advantage of every (legal) means for advancing your opportunities for success, and your speaking voice can play a strong role in creating that success.

Let Me Count the Ways

Libraries are well stocked with books that discuss what to say during a sales presentation. Our main concern here is not with content, but with the delivery of content. When you want to create trust, emphasize key selling points, and generate excitement, these Voice Power techniques will be a great asset. A resonant voice paves the way for a good relationship with a client. People listen longer to a voice they enjoy and are more likely to welcome it back for a repeat performance. Clear audible projection and a strong voice are by-products of a strong presence. The position of power supports good voice production and signals that you are a person to be taken seriously. Using your entire body when speaking gives the impression that you stand firmly behind what you say and that your commitment is strong. It builds trust.

Sales Inventory

There are many types of sales. You can sell a product, a service, or an idea. Some sales take place one-on-one. Sometimes, you will meet with a small group of company representatives, or make a sales presentation to a large group of district managers. There are hard sales, where your goal is to sell a specific item to a pre-qualified customer and conclude your business on the spot. And there are soft sales, which are more long-range and relationship-based. Selling when there is already a perceived need is different from creating a desire to buy where none existed before. A sales encounter can be quick and casual or formal and involved. Although fundamental similarities exist, of course, each of these situations has its own requirements and we must adjust the way we speak accordingly.

When we think of the word *sales*, perhaps what comes to mind are the formal one-on-one sales visits made to strangers, also called "cold calls." There is a reason they haven't been given a more attractive name. This type of selling is challenging because it requires careful planning and preparation if it is to be successful.

That is the first situation we are going to examine. You're there to sell a specific customer a specific product or service and to close the sale before you leave. Let's see how the Voice Power techniques we've learned can work to influence the outcome of this formal sales presentation. Maybe we can lead a horse to water *and* get him to drink.

What's the Problem?

My father used to say that all sales is about problem solving. You must determine in advance how what you offer solves your buyer's problems. Do your homework. Learn as much about your prospect and their business as possible and build on that information. Find out everything you can about your competitors and their weaknesses and strengths. Understand what makes your selling position unique. Know your product or service inside and out and the answers to questions a prospective buyer might ask. Anticipate objections and ways to counter them. If you can successfully communicate that you have a solution to their problem, many people are quite willing to let you take that problem off their hands so that they can move on to the next problem.

Now that you have determined which of your sales points are likely to be of most interest to this particular client, write them out in schematic form. Memorize and rehearse those points using all the voice delivery techniques we've covered. Concentrate on power pauses and money-word consonants that give special emphasis to anything you really want the client to digest and remember. Take time to record these practice sessions and study them until you find yourself so convincing that you start wondering if you shouldn't consider placing an order yourself.

The Warm-Up

This is a duet, but yours is the voice that plays the major role. Take your physical, mental, and vocal preparation as seriously as you would before giving a public speech. Before arriving at the appointment, make time to relax and center yourself with passive breathing. Like boxer Sugar Ray Leonard, visualize the entire encounter from beginning to end, always keeping your mind on the goal.

When your appointment is scheduled for early morning, it is important to eat something beforehand to get your throat muscles working. If your early meeting leaves you no time for breakfast—improvise. Imitate chewing and swallowing motions to wake up the muscles.

Just before arriving, try to find a private place for a quick warm-up to brush the cobwebs out of your voice. Sometimes you have to be a little creative to do this. If you know you're going to be in the company of others, you may have to do a good warm-up before you leave the house and practice a few unobtrusive **ZZ**s to reaffirm your support and resonance whenever you can. Your voice is one factor you *can* control in a sales duet. Make certain that yours is awake and warmed up.

Stream of Sales

In the many books available about selling techniques, you will find an abundance of good workable systems and useful formulas for the recommended sequence of a sales call. My father, who was the consummate career salesperson, liked to keep it simple—beginning, middle, and end.

The approach is to tell them who you are and get to know them. Then, present the material, making it clear that you are offering a solution that meets their needs. And finally, you negotiate a close. My father called it the "stream of sales."

Once, he explained it to me rather creatively in terms he felt that I, his music-loving daughter, could understand: "Start off with 'Getting to Know You' from *The King and I*, take them through that Kenny Rogers and Dolly Parton duet—the 'Islands in the Stream' of your sales points—and always keep in mind 'I Got You, Babe' [Sonny and Cher] is where you want to wind up."

In the Beginning

Like any duet, your exit depends in large part on your entrance. Using our musical analogy, people usually make their minds up by the first three notes. Your part at the beginning is to present yourself in the best possible light, to learn what makes the other person "tick," and to find common ground upon which to establish a relationship.

At this point, that person has no reason to care about you at all. Therefore, your first objective should be friendly chatter, in a warm, friendly, upbeat voice. This is how you get to know each other. It sets the tone for the entire encounter and can mean everything to the outcome of the visit. You must make people like you and *want* to buy from you or they'll never listen to your sales pitch.

The greeting sets the initial tempo of the exchange. This is where you first learn how the other person is likely to perform this duet. The tempo of their response sends a message about how your prospect wants this call to go and what they expect from this conversation. It will let you know how much they want to settle into it or move it along and get out.

Getting to Know You

Listen to your partner and take your tone from theirs. Variations in voice and delivery are strong signals of communication. People respond best to people who are like them. Start to read the client, match their style, and pace your voice accordingly. If they have a high voice, raise the pitch of your voice a little; if they speak quickly, speak more quickly yourself; if they speak slowly, you should slow down, too.

Sales are just like the rest of life. If you show people you are interested in them, they will be interested in you. Limit talking about yourself to just enough to let them know you are a person worth listening to. Your opening statements should indicate that, to you, a personal relationship is a top priority.

Concentrate on building trust. This is a good time for a warm voice and a tempo that encourages lingering. The more they open up and talk about themselves, the more stake they have in their relationship with you. As you get to know each other, the client is likely to talk about their problems and needs. Ask if there is an area in their business that is not going as well as it should be. This all-important information is fodder for your solution-based sales pitch.

In Tune With Your Subject

Be friendly, but not too familiar. Establish common ground, but establish your boundaries, too. It is fine to ask about their last vacation or what they're going to do during the holidays, but if you become too familiar, soon you're talking about Uncle Harry's dog and it distracts you both from the reason you're there. Everything you discuss should be in a positive tone of voice. When you give off good vibes, it's difficult for the other person not to give them back.

Humor and stories can play an important role. Laughing is a shared pleasure that helps you bond with your prospective customer. But use humor *only* if you can pull it off. Groaning should not be part of your prospect's response. Some people are like the prison inmate who couldn't get a laugh. If this is you, find another way to break the ice. But remember the commercial break. The real punch line is your sales pitch. Plan your stories so that they lead in to your sales pitch and help you to sell your product.

Around the Middle

These opening pleasantries are crucial for laying the foundation of the relationship and paving the way for your sale, but eventually you must get down to business and get to the sales pitch.

Sometimes you can take your cue from the prospect. Listen closely for changes in the other person's voice. You will hear when they are mentally checking their watch and are ready to move on. Often, it will be accompanied by abrupt shifts in their body position. But you can't always wait for a cue from them. Many people feel uncomfortable about the possibility of having to say no to someone they've recently met and have come to like. They'll avoid getting to the point by chatting about the Knicks long enough to run out of time. You must use signals from your own voice to maintain control.

Islands in the Stream

Lower the tone of your voice to indicate you are going to shift from personal to business. Let the buyer know that you're serious about your product and this meeting, but at the same time avoid being tense or abrupt. Lay out the main points of your sales presentation.

Build a convincing argument for the product or service you are offering, explaining how it meets the buyer's specific needs. Outline the areas where your product outshines the competition. Give the prospective buyer a new way to think about it. Present this as an opportunity to decide on a new issue, rather than trying to reverse a preexisting opinion.

The tone of your voice can modulate throughout your presentation to control the pace and flow of your material. Use consonants for clarity and accent, and to punch up key money words. Use the power pause for impact. Simple adjustments in speed, volume, and color make voice delivery one of your strongest selling tools. People tend to respond in similar fashion to the way you speak. Never let your voice project a negative quality. If you are really interested in the benefits to your client, it will show in your voice.

Take time to think about what the prospect is saying instead of only what you have to sell. Keep analyzing the client's pace, tone, style, and adjust to it, but don't forget that you have a part to play in this, too. Use what you know about color and variety to steer the duet in the direction you want it to take. Your partner may soon be adjusting their voice to yours.

Keep the Ball in the Air

Questions elicit better responses than statements. Lift the pitch of your voice to solicit answers. Talk less and listen more. As in any negotiating situation, creative silence draws out a prospective buyer. Give them room to express their concerns by leaving space for them to fill in. Listening encourages talking, and if you keep the other person talking as much as possible, they'll walk away thinking they've just had a brilliant conversation.

Speak respectfully about your competitors. Don't put down competitors because your prospect may have long-standing relationships with other companies. But *do* show prospective buyers how your product or service meets their needs better and how they will benefit from this new relationship. Concentrate on their agenda, not on your own. Review their needs. Make them feel you are extending them a service, not selling your product.

You must be alert for a sales call to change course at any moment. Passive breathing will keep you centered and focused on your part of the duet as well as where your partner is headed. It will also relax you. Tension is an energy vampire and a high level of positive energy is important in sales. Sometimes your energy must carry both you and the client when your duet partner's energy begins to falter.

Pay attention to what the other person says and how they say it. Remember, an objection is not necessarily a rejection. A rejection is not even always a rejection. However, don't keep talking if you see that the other person's mental receiver is off the hook. You don't have to be on the telephone to have a bad connection. You must know when to stop selling and ask for the sale.

Ask for the Sale

Yes, you've struck up a friendly rapport, but you both know why you're there. Summarize the prospect's needs, get them to agree that you have a solution, and then simply ask for the sale. Make your sales request concise and specific. At this point, there should be no question about what portion of the client's business you are looking to acquire. The tone of your voice should indicate that you are confident they will make the right decision.

You may want to apply more pressure here by raising the pitch and volume of your voice a bit. Get more intense. If you have a chair that moves, move it a few inches closer. Break through the other person's barrier. But be careful, if you choose to invade someone's personal space, you must adjust the volume and keep your voice down. You risk making your potential client uncomfortable if you invade both aural and visual protective space at the same time.

Don't forget to use one of the most powerful tools we have in a sales negotiation—the power of silence. Clients can't say "yes" if you don't give them *time* to say "yes."

Handling Rejection

Again, a big part of sales is knowing when to stop. You're not going to be successful 100 percent of the time, and sometimes you must accept that you are facing an immovable object and stop wasting your time and theirs. If you've tried everything you can think of, move on to greener pastures. As comedian W. C. Fields said, "Try, try, and try again. Then quit. There's no use being a damn fool about it."

It's okay to be disappointed. Prospective clients know you wouldn't be there if you weren't hoping to make the sale, but don't lay an angry guilt trip on them. Who wants to hear again from someone who makes them feel guilty? Maintain a positive tone of voice. Remember, your goal is to make clients feel good about themselves. There may be something that keeps a person from buying right now. You want to be able to go back because they may do business with you in the future.

Sometimes you can sense it's a lost cause from the beginning. If your prospect is having a bad day and taking it out on you instead of kicking the dog, they won't be budged. Learn when to fold. This is a good time to go straight to silence. Ed McMahon was right when he said that it is often best to just give a friendly smile and a wave of your hand and leave. Most people can't resist a parting retaliatory remark, so walking out without one puts you in a position of strength. This prospect may feel foolish when they're in a better mood the next day. The door may still be open.

I Got You, Babe

Let's say, instead, that all your planning and preparation has paid off. If you have been successful, *stop talking*. Once you've made the sale, there is no reason to continue, because there is only one other direction things can take now if you don't stop. And that is not where you want to go. Again, exercise the discipline of silence.

Of course, you should take a moment to confirm and reinforce the sale. But in your zeal to convince them that they have made the right decision, be sure you don't encourage them to reexamine that decision and change their mind when you're gone. No matter what the outcome, it takes courage to make the last word "silence."

Soft Sell

For many years I worked as the national sales director for David Horowitz Music Associates, a truly brilliant group of composers in New York City who write and record music for high-profile advertising campaigns. They've produced music for clients like Pepsi, Disney, IBM, M&Ms, Tums, Mercedes, and HBO. You've heard their work played on many a Super Bowl Sunday.

As their agent, I represented their services to the creative directors at major advertising agencies across the country, from Boston and Chicago to San Francisco. The type of selling that was required fell under the term *soft sales*, which is quite different from hard sales.

In soft sales, there may be an ongoing interest, but not always an immediate need. You're representing the idea of your integrity and the value of your company to a customer you hope will be inclined to look to you when the need arises.

Even if you do your homework and establish that they've used widgets in the past, in soft sales you have little way of knowing whether they've just used up the last widget and are ready to order more or have decided to do away with the machine that used the widgets altogether.

Advertising agencies closely guard the creative details of new ad campaigns, including the direction the music will take. There is no way to make a case for solving a specific problem or filling a need that will be decided—and filled—behind closed doors long before it is ever made public. My job was to convince my contacts at the agency to advocate on our behalf during the decision process. There is rarely an immediate payoff in this line of sales.

In soft sales, you need to concentrate on the relationship. Although it is a relationship that eventually leads to a sale, it is a relationship nevertheless. Chances are that you're going to be around for a while so you must make yourself real and memorable to the client. They must feel they benefit from time spent with you. Your voice should be one they look forward to hearing. Of course, there is the possibility you may get lucky and your visit will result in an immediate sale, but in soft sales your main concern is to present yourself and your company well and pave the way to be welcomed back.

Gather Together

On occasion you may meet with a small group of company representatives. Don't suddenly become an orator now that there is more than one person present. In fact, just the opposite: Your delivery should be more like it would be in a one-on-one situation. Keep the tone of your voice warm and personal. Concentrate on intimacy. One technique I teach my singers is to sing as if they were speaking intimately into the ear of one person. Focus on each individual independently as if you were alone with that person. Learn who they are and address them by name. Don't set yourself off from the group, rather become an integral part of it. If other people are sitting down, you should also sit. When you're all on the same level, it fosters the notion that you are one of them.

Let your voice inflection encourage frequent questions from *everyone*, so you can identify the principal decision-makers and the sources of possible objection. There will always be a group dynamic that exists among them. Be sensitive to it and take your cues from their interaction with each other. Sometimes, however, it is difficult to know where the real decision-making power rests. Many busy people rely heavily on the recommendations of staff, and that guy slouched in the corner wearing a T-shirt might just be the one you really need to convince.

Preaching to the Choir

The dynamics change when you present to a group of more than ten people. It's still a duet, only now your partner is an entire chorus. Gone is the opportunity for intimacy that is possible with a small group or one-on-one. Your voice must project your personal power, your confidence in yourself, and your belief in what you are offering.

You may or may not have sound equipment to assist you, so prepare your voice for a large sales presentation as you would for a speech. Use good full-body support and a resonant, committed tone of voice that reaches out to include everyone present.

If you find the situation dictates that you must be seated during your sales pitch, you can still use your legs and lower body for support. Try this. Sit forward in your chair, and shift to the side so you're seated in the twelve o'clock to three o'clock quadrant, with one leg in front and the other off to the side and a little behind you. Press into the floor and balance lightly on the balls of your feet—so you would still be in place if someone pulled the chair out from under you. It's like posting on a horse. This will help you engage the support you need to carry your message to the back of the room.

In essence, you're on the podium here and should apply all the techniques you would use to make any speech more powerful and effective—power pauses for emphasis and long consonants to drive home the money words. If you fail to use the tools you have for controlling the flow of information, it's like having the answers to the test and not using them.

Universal Sales

Oprah Winfrey once said, "Luck is a matter of preparation meeting opportunity." In sales, good preparation dramatically increases the odds of success. Your presentation should never be spontaneous, but should always *sound* as if it were. Use the principles of contrast and variety to put punch and power into your sales duet. Modulate your voice to fit the tone and rhythm of the situation and to create a bond with your prospect. Plan out your part and visualize theirs. Above all, in this duet, endeavor to let your speaking voice convey graciousness at all times. It was French writer/philosopher Albert Camus who said, "Charm is a way of getting the answer yes without having asked any clear question."

CHAPTER NINE

Voice Mail
Theater

".. . SO LEAVE *a message when you hear the BEEP!"*

Okay, now what? It was William Shakespeare who said, "All the world's a stage," and, boy, are we ever on it with voice mail! Once you leave that message, you can't take it back. It's on your "permanent record." By the time you hear the beep, it's too late to start thinking about what you're going to say.

It's not like cutting a record where you can record multiple versions of the same song, and later paste up the best parts. In the recording studio, you can always go back and redo an entire section or "punch in" just one word. No, voice mail is more like being recorded live at Nightmare Studios where there is only one chance to get it right. You're stuck with whatever message you left the first time—for *anyone* to hear.

We're not concerned here about a quick call to your best friend, but rather the call that absolutely must count—when you think your future comfort might depend on the impression you leave. Maybe it's a call to your attorney, the call that could close a sale, or a call to a prospective employer—the VIP calls. We're performing on tape and we had better make it good because now it's in someone else's hands and there is no taking it back.

Think back. What was the worst message you ever left? Does it still make you cringe?

> "Hi, um, Mr. Smith. This is Jim. Um, I was wondering, um, if you had decided, um, if you had, um, decided on that, that, was it a sales position? If you could, um, let me know. . . ."

Of course, there is always wishful thinking. Maybe it didn't record? Maybe the tape will break? Maybe somebody will record over it by mistake?

And, yes, some systems do offer to let you go back and take another stab at it. *"To erase and rerecord your message, press three."* But does it *really* erase the first one? That's what I always wonder. Is it a trap? Later that day, will they stand around listening to me trying to get it right, over and over again?

It's easy to see why the *BEEP!* strikes fear into the hearts of the bravest individuals. It's an unforgiving record of our thoughts on tape. And now, because of Caller ID, if you decide two rings into a call that you're not prepared, you can't just hang up. They'll know you've called—you're busted no matter what.

Buffy Does Her Nails

But what is even scarier than voice mail? What is scarier is leaving your precious message with Buffy the Message Slayer. It's Buffy the breathing, but definitely disinterested, third party on the other end. You have no control over how she is going to interpret your message. It's like the game of gossip. There is a much greater chance she'll get it wrong than get it right.

> "Please tell Mr. Smith that Carol Jones called. I just moved to Detroit from Kalamazoo, where I recently passed the bar exam. I would really like to work for your law firm. Is there a time we could meet to discuss this? Please ask him to call me at 1-800-467-0490."

Buffy turns this into:

> "Joan Carol. Wants job. Used to work at the zoo. Will meet you at the bar."

Of course, this is assuming Buffy actually writes down the message. How many times have you left a long, detailed message with someone like Buffy, only to find out later that all she wrote down was your name? And got *that* wrong, too? But don't blame Buffy. How do *you* take messages for other people? That's right. Just as fast as you can. You don't want to write a dissertation either, do you? You just want to get it done and get back to what you were doing.

So, is voice mail better than leaving your message with a human? You bet. People say they hate voice mail, but I would much rather leave a message on voice mail than with Buffy any day.

Voice Mail in Business

When I worked in the music rep business, I figured my clients probably received more than fifty calls a day from sales reps like me. Most of them would have liked to talk to everyone who called, but who has time? Busy people live and breathe voice mail—and with good reason. In this increasingly *un*private world, voice mail is a way to get some small measure of privacy by allowing us to select which calls we want to answer. Of course, this works both ways.

I'll never forget the chill that came over me the first time I reached a client's voice mail. I was calling Robin Sherman at the advertising agency of Earle Palmer Brown in Baltimore. It's etched in my brain and the moment still haunts me. *Wait, Shhhhhh! Wait a minute, I thought. Don't let this get around. Pleeeeease!* I had this horrible premonition that if everyone figured out they could use voice mail to dodge their calls it would change the whole way business was done by telephone. And I was right. The odds of reaching a breathing human seem to diminish every year.

But voice mail can be a great time-saver. An appropriate message can tie up loose ends. You can confirm an appointment, leave detailed instructions or specifications, or say your piece and get on with your life. Maybe you will even get lucky and conclude the business with a quick effective message that completes a round of telephone tag. *(Or should that be telephone "tackle"?)*

So now, I expect to reach voice mail. And when I do, I use that moment to leave a brief message that brings me one step closer to that person and the conclusion of our business together.

Voice Mail Approval Rating

How does your voice mail performance rate? Let's imagine you have recently been on a job interview. You *want* this job. Go to a telephone other than your own. Imagine you're calling the person who interviewed you. Leave a message for that person on your own personal voice mail. Then listen back to the message carefully.

* Was the sound of your voice appealing?
* Did you sound nervous or confident?
* Did you sound professional?
* Was the message precise and to the point?
* Did you ask for specific action?
* Did your message invite closure?
* Did you state your vital information clearly and repeat it so that the interviewer knew who you were and how to reach you? Remember, *you* know your telephone number by heart, the receiver does not.

Listen to your message again and list five positive things about it. For example, you might comment:

* I sounded confident without sounding smug.
* I didn't say "um" or stumble over my words.
* I sounded prepared, but not rehearsed.
* I covered everything I wanted to say.
* I remembered to leave my telephone number.

Now list five negative things about your message. You need to work on your voice mail skills if your answers resemble any of the following:

* My thoughts seemed scattered.
* I stumbled over my words.
* I think I might have called my prospective boss "Um."
* My voice cracked several times. Do I really sound like that?
* I forgot to leave my name.

Well, how did you do? Would your message encourage this person to: (a) hire you; (b) forget you; or (c) get a restraining order?

Now rate your message on a scale of 1 to 10, with 10 being "I can name my own salary," and 1 being "Maybe working in a car wash will be good for my tan."

Save the message that you have recorded. At the end of this chapter, you're going to leave another message and compare the two.

Be Prepared

When the call really matters, good preparation guarantees that you will leave the most concise and effective message possible. It boils down to content and delivery. Since you always stand a good chance of reaching voice mail, here is how to prepare for your big recording moment.

Let's look at the big picture first. To say what you actually want to say, you have to first know what you want to say. Think about what you want to achieve with this call. Why are you calling in the first place? Do you want this person to call you back? Maybe, but it's wasting a hello if that is your only concern. Instead of simply leaving your name and number, view this call as a chance to advance your cause, whatever it may be. This is an excellent opportunity to do more than merely receive a callback—but only if you know what you want to accomplish and plan on how to accomplish it.

You can use voice mail as an opportunity for selling your ideas to the other person, providing more details about your product, or stressing the benefits of your service. Note how much the following caller accomplishes with this interactive message:

> "Hello, Mr. Trump. This is Carol Jones with Elegant Interiors. My number is 1-800-467-0490. It was a pleasure meeting you yesterday, and I want to say that if you choose Elegant Interiors to redecorate your casino, I'll do everything in my power to make the pro-

cess easy for you. I know you have a very busy schedule, but if you could spare a few minutes to return my call, I have some ideas I think you'll find very interesting. My number again is 1-800-467-0490. Thank you, Mr. Trump."

See how much information she packed into a few seconds? It all begins in the planning stages, prior to picking up the telephone. Before you make that all-important call, organize and prioritize your information by following these six steps:

Six-Step Program:

1. Jot down one line that clearly states what you would most like to see accomplished, changed, put into motion, or concluded by your message. Now, thinking in both broad and specific terms, write out what you want to accomplish. You may have a specific purpose for making the call as well as a broader objective. If you're calling to make an appointment for a job interview, your specific goal may be: "I want to set up an appointment for an interview on Friday." And your broader goal may be: "I want this call to help me land this job." Always ask yourself how you can get the most mileage out of your message.

2. Gather documents or information that you may need to have at hand when making the call. Perhaps you're going to need a product serial number or an invoice number. You may need the notes from your last meeting or telephone conversation, prices, your schedule, or the new specifications.

3. Organize your message into a well-planned sequence of topics in the order of their importance. One of the tricky

things about voice mail is that you never know how long you'll have to talk. It's like standing on a trap door. Will you have thirty seconds to say your piece? Or will you reach a voice-activated machine that lets you go on and on? But what happens if you pause too long with a voice-activated system?

> "Hi Joe, it's Sharon, I'm between flights. You wouldn't believe the meal they served us on the plane. I think it was Hot Dog Helper! It was just too gross to eat so I'm really hungry and looking forward to having a great meal when you pick me up. So anyway, I'm coming in on flight # . . . , let's see . . . *BEEP!*"

If you stop to gather your thoughts in the middle of your message, you may get cut off. Some busy people allow only a few seconds for callers to record their messages, so state the most important facts up front: name, company, and telephone number. For example, *"This is Joe Jones from the WIDGET company. My number is 1-800-467-0490."*

Make certain you say your telephone number clearly and distinctly, leaving enough time for the other person to write it down. It's annoying to have to play a message three or four times to make out the phone number. There are people who simply won't bother to do this and your message may be lost on them. Repeat the number if possible.

Leave your full name. Don't make your listener guess who you are from among the dozens of calls they may have had that day. *"Hi, this is Dave."* Okay, now what does that mean? I know eleven Daves well enough for each one of them to think I might recognize his voice. It's rather pretentious not to leave your last name, unless you happen to be Oprah, Sting, or Madonna.

Or how about this one: *"Hi, it's me."* People assume because *they* know who they are that you do, too. And when you identify your-self, it's stronger to announce, *"This is Renee Grant-Williams"* than *"My name is Renee Grant-Williams."* *"My name is . . ."* sounds like you're the household pet. *"Hello, my name is Sparky."* Actually, *"My name is . . ."* seems like it should be followed by a confession of some sort. *"My name is Renee Grant-Williams and I'm a shopaholic."* Be a person—not a name.

4. Ask for a specific action. Don't make the person you're calling guess what you want. Make your request specific and clear by using voice color, consonants, and rhythm to highlight the most important issues. In the following message, note how the caller specifies the actions she wants Mr. Smith to take, while emphasizing the time frame.

> "Hello, Mr. Smith. This is Carol Jones, catering coor-dinator for Seaside Inn. My number is 1-800-467-0490, extension 2. I'm calling to get a final head count for your awards banquet, October 14. The catering department needs that information confirmed by no later than October 10. If I happen to be out of the office when you call back, please leave a message on my voice mail telling me how many people you expect to attend. That number again is 1-800-467-0490, ex-tension 2. Thanks. I look forward to hearing from you about the final head count by the tenth."

5. Now we can sit back and wait for the return call, right? Sorry, but if you expect to have your first call returned automatically, you must be living on some planet that I've never heard of. The reality is that many people, probably even you, don't respond to every message in a timely fash-ion. One way to prioritize incoming voice mail might be to compose an outgoing message something like this:

"If you think your call is more important than anyone else's, dial 1 now. If you've forgotten why you made this call, press the memory key. If you suffer from feelings of inferiority, please hang up and free the line for someone who really matters."

Be patient. Realize that your message is not the only message this person will receive today. And you might not be at the top of their list. If the VIP you're trying to reach doesn't return your first call, don't let it drop there; most people usually don't mind if you call again. The following tricks of the trade can pave the way for you to call back without being labeled a pest. Maybe you'll even get your call returned.

Let your VIPs know that you understand how busy their lives are by always giving them an out for not returning your call. Nobody likes to feel guilty. They're much more likely to call back if they don't feel they are going to be scolded. Instead of whining, *"You know, I've called you four times already and you haven't called me back!"* use something like, *"Sounds like you're busy this week. If you're not able to get back to me, I'll try to catch you next week."* Or you might include something like: *"I'll check back with you early tomorrow afternoon if you don't reach me today."*

Because you may need to leave several messages for the same person, develop a shorthand system of notes to help you remember what you have said on previous calls. Be prepared to shuffle your chat around so your messages will sound fresh and spontaneous. We tend to fall into the same few catch phrases, such as "Hope you're doing well," "Hope business is good," "Hope the family's fine," and "Hope I don't say 'hope' again."

6. Eventually, you have to end this time-consuming, back-and-forth calling. Ask yourself whether there is a way to conclude your business with one well-thought-out mes-

sage. For example, you can use a voice mail message to finalize meeting arrangements: *". . . and I will see you then at 4:30 tomorrow afternoon, Thursday, the fourth."*

You'll want to know whether they've received your message and are in agreement, so leave a callback number and ask for confirmation: *"Please call me at 1-800-467-0490 to confirm."* They can let you know by machine that they got your final answer. *"I got your message about changing our meeting time from 1:00 to 4:30 and that's just fine with me. So I'll see you at 4:30 on Thursday, the fourth, at your office."* Now you can both move on to other things.

A word of caution: Know when to stop talking. Don't keep rambling on and on just because the tape is still running. Remember, you are taking up their time. We've all had messages that were so lengthy and convoluted that we fast-forwarded through them or erased them before they ended. Does this sort of thing sound familiar?

"Hello, Mrs. Smith. This is George Davis. I was supposed to meet with you tomorrow morning for the 911-operator job interview. But I took my car in for maintenance today, and they promised me they'd have it back to me by late afternoon. But now the mechanic says the 'pinging' isn't just a loose bolt after all, and he wants to put in a whole new transmission. Yeah, right, like I have the money for that! So I took it somewhere else to get a second opinion, but they won't even be able to look at it till late tomorrow afternoon, so anyway, to make a long story shor . . . !"

It's too late for that now. There could have been important information in there, but who would want to wade through all the chitchat to find out? Your message will be appreciated if it is brief and to the point. If someone asks you for the time, don't tell them how to build a watch.

Adjust Your Attitude

Once you have a firm grip on your information, it is time to adjust your attitude. And by that, I don't mean it's time for happy hour. I'm suggesting that you put yourself in the proper frame of mind for the call by adjusting your mood, your humor, your spirit, your approach, and your outlook on life. We are not one-dimensional creatures, yet we are going to leave a permanent record of our attitude and intentions on voice mail.

When a singer comes into my voice studio to work on a song, I always ask: "Who are you singing this song to? Is it to your love interest? Your mother? A buddy? Your best friend?" Depending on the relationship, the attitude and personal energy are going to be different. I have my singers visualize the other person and how they hope that person will respond. We can do the same thing when we leave a voice mail message.

Visualizing what you want from this message can make a difference in how it plays out for you. Let's say that you are making a call requesting urgent information. Your project is at a standstill until you receive this information. Before you make the call, envision the results you want from the call. Because you need the information immediately, the message requires a firm tone. Be polite, but firm.

> "Our shipping department hasn't yet received the fax from you with the exact number of widgets you wish to purchase. I'm certain you're anxious to get that merchandise, but your order is on hold until we receive those figures. It is important that you get that information to me so that I can ship the order out to you."

In your mind, see yourself receiving the information quickly and easily. When you call, these positive visualizations will be reflected in the tone of your voice. Who knows? You might even receive the information the shipping department needs.

Not all messages are urgent. You may be excited because you recently closed a major deal and you want your new client to catch your upbeat attitude. Imagine that the person receiving your call is as energized and excited as you are. Let the tone of your voice reflect your attitude and expectations.

Use a tone that is appropriate to the relationship, but keep it human. You may be talking to a machine, but your message will be heard by a person. Mentally punch through to the image of that person and make them absolutely clear in your mind. Speak to the person—*not* to the machine. You must project *through* the machine.

One way to create the proper attitude in your voice is to dress for the occasion. This may sound silly considering that we are, after all, talking *into* a machine that talks *onto* a machine before it ever gets to a person. However, take the following advice from a performance coach: It doesn't matter that they can't see you. *You* can see you. Dress well and sit tall. It's hard to sell yourself as a go-getter when it's one o'clock in the afternoon and you're still in your bunny slippers.

According to legend, theatrical producer Florenz Ziegfeld of the Ziegfeld Follies used to buy silk undergarments for his dancers. His accountant couldn't understand spending so much money on something that no one was going to see. "Who's going to know?" he asked. Ziegfeld insisted that the girls would know, and that it would show in their performances.

I ask the singers I work with to dress according to the image they want to project when they go into the studio to record. Whenever they dress like stars, they seem to sound more like stars. Leaving voice mail is like recording in a miniature studio, so set the stage for yourself and dress for the occasion.

The expression on your face when you leave a message projects through the machine. Some people leave voice mail messages with about as much enthusiasm as calling in sick to work. There is no rule requiring that you must smile all the time. But if you want to convey an upbeat attitude, you should smile—we'll hear it in your voice. After all, if you're a successful person, chances are that you have something to smile about.

It is impressive to watch an accomplished singer of commercial jingles at work. These people are well paid to act thrilled with the products they promote—and you can hear it in their voices. When they're singing an upbeat jingle, they usually have big, happy smiles on their faces. The moment they finish singing, the smiles disappear. However, once the next take begins, the smiles are back in place because these pros know we can hear the difference.

Adjust Your Voice

One of the most important aspects of leaving a powerful message is the sound of your voice. Many people say that they are uncomfortable hearing the sound of their own voice. What about you? How would you feel about spending ten years on a deserted island with someone who sounded exactly like you? Your voice is about to represent you on a permanent recording, so use everything you've learned in previous chapters to make your delivery clear and the tone of your voice sound rich, full, and confident—a voice *you* would like to hear.

Your Outgoing Message

Once you know how to leave effective voice mail messages for other people, it's time to evaluate your outgoing message. How does it stack up? Does it meet our criteria for a good message that covers all the bases? Tone and delivery are important here, too. Do you sound like someone you would like to meet? What do you want to change?

We are many things to many people, which makes it difficult to record a message that you would want both your boss and your best friend to hear. Remember, every single person who calls when you're not available is going to hear what you say. To be on the safe side, choose the one person in the world you would most like to impress—or *hate* to offend—and imagine you are talking directly to that person. This trick will help you to make the right choices and set a tone that covers all the bases.

Whatever you do, avoid the robot voice so many people use for their outgoing message. My mother has one of those messages. "Hello · this · is · the · Jan · sen · residence." I keep waiting to hear, *"We · are · the · Cone · heads. · We · are · from · France."* Always try to sound like yourself, or at least the self you'd like to be. Speak clearly and distinctly. Don't rush and don't run your words together—but don't turn into a Conehead either.

Gauge your message to the attitude of your business. A flip and clever message is a bad idea—*"Are we out of the office or just ignoring YOU?"*—unless it is appropriate to your business and you're very good at comedy. You are more likely to get away with a creative message if you're the owner of a balloon store than if you are working at a financial institution. *"Thank you for calling ABC Bank. We lost interest and closed down for the day."* People don't like to joke about their money. And if you receive business calls at home, never let your child record the outgoing message: *"My mommy's not here . . .* (sound of baby babbling)." Only immediate family members find it adorable.

Since our world is full of people who have short attention spans, keep your message short. No long music intros, please. If people want to hear music, they can turn on the radio. They might not feel like listening to Mozart or Metallica at that moment.

OGM Recording Studios

The following tips can help you to produce a clear recording. Because the microphones in ordinary message systems are low fidelity, you need to move close to the machine's microphone when recording your message to add presence and warmth to your voice. But not too close because a volume spike can overload the capacity of the microphone, which causes the sound to break up and distort. Also, nobody needs to hear your dog bark or the theme music of an "Andy Griffith Show" rerun in the background—so plan ahead for quiet.

Write a script for your outgoing message before you record it and be sure to identify yourself by name or telephone number. Re-record and review your message until you're happy with the way it represents you. Unlike leaving messages for other people, here we have a chance to redo our less-than-perfect takes.

Your New Rating

To see how much you have learned so far, repeat the steps you took at the beginning of this chapter. Leave another message for your imaginary job interviewer. Remember, you really *want* this job, so leave a message that will help you get it. This time use all the techniques and tips you have learned.

Now listen back and critique your new message. How do you rate your performance? Write down five positive things about the message and five areas that could still be improved. When you compare this new version to the earlier message, do you hear a difference? Have you left a stronger, more positive image of yourself? What improvements do you observe in the overall impression of your new message? If you don't feel your original message would have helped you to get that job, is the second message more likely to get you hired? Rate your message on a scale of 1 to 10.

Press Rewind

Every time you make an important telephone call, it is a step into the unknown. If you still question why all this preparation is necessary for a voice mail message, it is because the payoff can be substantial. Think of it as a timesaving device. Start planning your calls so that you will leave a lasting, positive impression that gets your calls returned and your business concluded.

Sure, voice mail can be scary, but you don't need to panic when you hear an answering machine beep. Make voice mail your friend. The next time you hear the beep, let that sound be your cue to leave a powerful, clear, personalized message.

> "This is Renee Grant-Williams. My number is 1-800-467-0490. I just wanted to let you know how much I enjoyed working with you and that I'm looking forward to our next chapter together."

CHAPTER TEN

Success Appeal at Work

MY FRIEND Ronda is a computer systems trouble-shooter who used to own a thriving temp agency in New York. One reason for its success was that she personally went to every job site so she could analyze the workforce already in place and send the appropriate person out to augment it.

Her contention was that most offices have at least one overlooked talent. On one job, she was enormously impressed with an eighteen-year-old employee who was smart, capable, and a natural whiz with computers. Ronda recommended that the company put this kid in charge of supervising the systems. She was a beautiful girl, tall and slim, with an elegant way about her.

But when she opened her mouth, it was all over. It wasn't only that she had a Brooklyn accent, but her loud voice emphasized it. Ronda was amazed to hear such a voice coming from a girl who looked so delicate. This is not a success story. The company couldn't get beyond the voice and this kid didn't get the promotion she deserved. All that my friend's glowing recommendation earned for the girl was an increase in responsibility and an extra workload. She languished for years at the bottom of the office food chain. That voice would always hold her back.

Up the Ladder

Good vocal skills are not only essential for jobs that require giving speeches or sales presentations, they are, in fact, important in every type of business and at every level. Even in positions not generally considered to be voice-intensive, the way we speak has a direct effect on our opportunities for advancement. You must be a good communicator if you want success in any field. I've sketched out a hypothetical work scenario so that we can see what an important role the voice plays at every stage.

Career Decision

Assess your natural talents and choose a career you're suited for. If your speaking skills are questionable, it is probably not a good idea to seek a career in broadcast journalism. But remember, good speaking skills are required in most professions. Teachers, salespeople, lawyers, coaches, receptionists, executives, small business owners, training consultants, politicians, and ministers have all opted for careers that are voice-intensive.

Unfortunately, there is little training available to help young people develop the speaking skills they need. And, yes, I'm probably getting up on my soapbox here, but I would love to see schools and colleges create programs that address this issue so that graduates looking for work in a competitive marketplace would be armed with every advantage.

Selling Yourself

In order to be successful at a job, you must first *get* the job. The hardest sales job of all is selling yourself. There is a great deal of personal validation at stake. If you fail in your efforts to sell a product, you can always blame it on the product. However, when you're selling yourself, it all comes down to you and what you communicate about yourself. I don't know that I've ever heard anyone say, "He's a really poor communicator, let's hire this guy."

Do your homework by learning everything you can about the company, its products or services, the requirements of the position, and the duties that will fall to you. Develop a clear idea of why you are the perfect candidate for this position and why you want it. Be realistic about the skills and qualifications you bring to the job. Anticipate questions you are likely to be asked and rehearse your responses. Visualize the outcome you desire.

The way your voice represents you is an important one-third of the impression you make. You must prepare your body, brain, and voice for a job interview exactly as you would for any other sales call. Of course, it all starts with the breathing—breathing to reduce stress, battle nerves, and center yourself, as well as to trigger the support system that ensures your voice remains steady and confident. Don't forget to warm up your body so that you appear energized and fresh. If you run through a few vocal exercises before arriving at the interview, your technique will kick in to help you produce a warm and committed speaking voice.

Indicate that getting the right job, not just any job, is important to you. The tone of your voice should register enthusiasm for learning more about the company, the position, and the opportunities for advancement. Ask questions frequently. Listen carefully so that you can learn as much about the potential employer as they learn about you.

Silence is golden. Don't volunteer information that is not requested unless you're absolutely certain that it will advance your cause. The interviewer will be asking questions and discussing issues that are important to the employer. There is no point in muddying up the waters by diverting attention to areas of your life and personal history that are of little consequence to the position for which you are interviewing.

Use consonants to punch up the positive aspects of your qualifications and work history. Communicate the skills you bring to the table and stress the positive contribution your presence will bring to this company. Choose your words carefully. When interviewing new employees, my stepfather always gave more serious consideration to applicants who claimed they were "looking for work," as opposed to those who came in merely "looking for a job."

During the interview, you must endeavor to communicate personal credibility and strive to bond with the person conducting the interview. Pacing is important here; an interviewer will respond more favorably to someone they can relate to easily. The interviewer may be hiring you to work for someone else, but they must like and trust you enough to believe you will make the interviewer look good for recommending you.

Job Survival

So, let's say you get the job you want. Chances are there are going to be coworkers involved. As one of the principal definitions of the word *politics*, *Webster's Dictionary* lists "competition between competing interest groups or individuals for power and leadership." It might be said that where more than one are gathered, there will always be politics. As you will be spending many of your waking hours in the presence of these people; it is important to establish your place in the pecking order from the very beginning. You only have one chance to make a first impression.

Make sure your voice is a welcome addition to the workplace dynamic by fitting in with the style and pace of the company. Just as you might dress differently for a managerial position with a blue-chip company like IBM than you would for a position with a more freewheeling and laid-back company like Apple, you must be sensitive to the prevailing dynamic and your voice must reflect that you fit in.

Always come back to the overriding goal, which is to make people listen. If you talk too fast, too slow, too loud, or too soft, people don't listen to you and don't remember what you have said. A shrill voice puts others on edge and drives them away as surely as one that is set on permanent whine. Use lower abdominal breathing and support to control the quality of your voice. Make good use of variety and inflection, fashioning the delivery of your words to suit each immediate situation.

Think before you speak. As a general rule—but especially when you are the new person—it is better to say too little than too much. Listening is usually more productive than talking. Learn all you can about other people before revealing yourself to them. Even then—be careful. Fly below the office radar. What others know about you may be used against you.

I'd like to say a word about gossip, and that word is *don't*. The same applies to situations of conflict between coworkers. While it may be tempting to involve yourself in the affairs of others, "if," as they say, "you don't have a dog in the fight, stay out of it." Silence is golden.

Use what you know about breathing to control your emotions and nerves when things get tense. Thomas Jefferson wisely suggested, "When angry, count to ten before you speak. If very angry, count to one hundred." Be firm, but polite. Under no circumstance should profanity be part of your office vocabulary.

The Working Woman

Throughout the past few decades, women have begun to emerge as an equal force in business. Although complete equality still does not exist between the sexes (in 1999, women's earnings were still only approximately 70 percent of men's earnings), every year women make strides toward parity in the workplace. This has presented some interesting dilemmas for all concerned. The challenge for women has been how to project authority without losing femininity; the challenge for men has been to gracefully adjust to the reversal of traditional roles.

What type of voice is appropriate for the workplace? Do women need to project masculine authority traits to be successful? It might have seemed that way when women adopted power suits and big shoulder pads in the 1980s. It took a couple of decades for women to realize that they didn't need to disguise themselves as men to hold a job.

Women bring an entirely different set of skills to the workplace. Because women are physically smaller by nature than their male counterparts, they have always had to rely on persuasion and compromise rather than on power and force. It is not necessary for women to sound like men, but women could benefit from incorporating some successful male traits into their business style.

To establish their authority, women must project it through a voice that is clear and confident. A woman doesn't need to speak in an unnaturally low voice to command respect, but using a somewhat lower-pitched voice sounds better than using one that is high-pitched and shrill. Women should concentrate on mellow tones, supporting well from the lower body so that the chest cavity is free to resonate. The result should sound warm and wise, not mannish.

Women seem to be more open to their emotional side, as one of the by-products of millennia of child rearing. But working women must find a way to keep those emotions from taking over on the job. When the pressure is on, women can use passive breathing to stay relaxed and centered. Support is important here, too. By keeping the production of one's voice centered in the strongest part of the body and away from the throat, the voice will sound steady and calm. Nervousness and uncertainty are more likely to register in an unsupported voice.

Women should keep extraneous motion in both word and gesture to a minimum. Meaningless gestures are distracting. It has been said that women play with their hair to diffuse the seriousness of what they are saying. Men don't embellish. Lunch? Sure. Women should talk to men the way men talk to them. Say what you mean and stop talking. Don't keep on selling after the point has been sold.

Sexual Harassment

The manner in which you deliver your words can help you to avoid sexual harassment or the charge of sexual harassment. I won't presume to tell you how to choose your words to avoid becoming embroiled in this problem, but I can tell you that vocal inflection plays a large part in the way intentions register. That business about saying the same thing, but coming across differently, is especially important here.

One of your best defenses is to use your voice to project a professional image at all times, while making certain that you're not giving the wrong signals. You must use vocal inflection to indicate the difference between a well-meaning compliment and a come-on. Similar words delivered with a lilt to the voice and a nervous giggle could send the wrong cue.

People tend to prey on the weak, which makes sense, because it's hard work preying on the strong. A steady, confident voice signals that you are not a person to be taken lightly. Concentrate on using a professional tone that is assured and clear, and it is unlikely your words will be misconstrued.

Telephone Etiquette

With no visual clues to aid you, business conducted over the telephone is especially dependent on vocal inflection. This is another place where the sensitivities you develop as a verbal duet partner will be useful. Use your listening skills to gauge the pace of the conversation and to interpret silence on the other end of the telephone line. Speak clearly, using consonants to punch up important words and frequent pauses to invite response. Visualize the person you're talking to and imagine projecting yourself *through* the mouthpiece.

In fact, all the basic principles of voice mail preparation and delivery discussed in Chapter 9 apply to business transacted by telephone. And I'd like to add one more thought here about telephone etiquette. In some fields, such as real estate, you must make yourself available to clients during non-business hours. If you receive business calls at home, be vigilant about maintaining the perception of professionalism. Have an additional telephone line installed and make certain the kids understand that this telephone is off-limits to them. Establish a privacy zone where you can talk business without excusing yourself to settle a dispute about who is going to put the dishes away.

Job Endurance

Throughout your work life, you will spend a large portion of your waking hours on the job—successful people rarely work only a forty-hour week. Tension generated on the job can take a toll on your body, brain, and voice. If you notice that you are spending more time than you care to admit zoning out in front of the television set, like a couch potato with a remote control implant, it is time for a change. You must take steps to cut fatigue and boost your energy level. By eliminating tension from your body during the day, you'll have more energy to devote to family and friends at the end of it.

Body, Brain, and Voice

For energy and endurance, I'm afraid it comes back to exercise. Make a committed investment in regular exercise and it will pay off. Taking breaks throughout the day to stretch will help keep your body limber. Get up and walk around the office, or better yet, around the block. Stretch your mind. Give yourself a break from what you are doing and spend ten minutes reading a book or an article that interests you. Or use this time to learn ten more words of another language—anything to take you off your work path for a few minutes so that you can come back reenergized and fresh.

Remember to make time for a few StressBuster breathing breaks. Using the strong muscles of your lower body takes a tremendous amount of pressure off your neck and throat, but as we grow tired, we forget to engage the body for support. Low breathing will remind you to transfer the tension from up around your neck and shoulders to your lower body so that you can use it to support your voice.

Ravages of the Road

Many people who travel frequently by air find themselves struggling with their voices after landing. This is a common problem for singers when they begin to tour. When you travel in any capacity, you must deal with a variety of things over which you have little control, such as temperature, humidity, climate, and changes in altitude and air pressure.

Anyone who travels for business knows the importance of being in top shape when working in unfamiliar surroundings. The better you feel about your body and your voice, the more successful your trip will be. A few tips I've picked up working with singers will help you overcome the special difficulties of being on the road.

Travel can be exhausting, so it is important to include rest and regrouping time in your schedule. Get more sleep than you normally would. You're likely to be sedentary for long periods of time when you're traveling, so stretch frequently. Schedule time for exercise and actually follow through with your program—this is not a good time to break from your regular routine.

Maintain a consistent level of energy by eating lightly during the day. Skip the two martinis at lunch, but don't skip meals. Carry healthy snacks or energy bars. If you're headed to an altitude that is significantly different from your current one, or are traveling across many time zones, you may want to arrive a few days early to give your body time to adjust.

The stress of travel, combined with exposure to other travelers in close proximity, leaves your immune system vulnerable and puts you at risk for illness. There is no way to know for certain what to expect from the temperature of the environment in which you will find yourself. Be prepared for temperature fluctuations by having options; take clothing you can layer to avoid becoming chilled or overheated.

Lack of adequate moisture is a big problem when we travel. It's a good idea to carry bottled water if you aren't accustomed to drinking the local tap water. Also, it may be a while before the flight attendants get to your row, so take a bottle or two on board to help counteract jet lag. (*Why is it we catch a "plane," but get "jet" lag? Why not "catch a jet" or "get plane lag"?*)

Those of us who spend a fair amount of time traveling have experienced how drying hotel room heat can be, so I highly recommend taking along a travel-sized humidifier and using it at night in your room to keep body and voice moist and healthy. There are a number of portable humidifiers available that are light enough for travel. Or try this: Turn on the hot water in the shower and let it run. The steam will clean your sinuses while taking the wrinkles out of your clothes.

In short, when you travel, you must protect yourself and your voice by planning ahead. Allow time in your schedule for adequate rest and exercise. Eat light, regular meals. Maintain a constant body temperature by packing clothing that can be layered. And get plenty of moisture inside and out.

Foreign Exchange

I would like to elaborate on the discussion in Chapter 5 about doing business with international organizations. When you travel abroad for business and are not familiar with the language, take time to learn a few phrases as a courtesy to your host country. Don't worry, you don't need to be flawless for the gesture to be appreciated. During the Cold War, President John F. Kennedy charmed the world when he spoke the words "Ich bin ein Berliner" at the Berlin Wall. Part of the charm was that he had unwittingly stumbled onto a colloquialism when he declared, "I am a Berliner." How was he to know that "Berliner" also meant "doughnut" in the local dialect?

Once I was asked to conduct a series of seminars in Argentina. I was familiar with the other Romance languages, but had never studied Spanish, so I was relieved to learn I was not expected to be fluent in the language because a simultaneous translation would be provided. I did, however, memorize a dozen or so Spanish terms that were central to my message and sprinkled those liberally throughout my presentations. As my first event rolled along, I was feeling rather satisfied with my efforts. I could see the audience responding, they were smiling and nodding. Afterward, I was crushed when Fabiola, my translator, came up and told me they wanted to know why I was speaking to them in Italian.

When you're conducting business with Asian partners, you may encounter another situation where effort is more important than expertise. Don't be surprised when the meetings are over and your hosts are ready for an evening of karaoke. Uh, oh. What now? Karaoke may not be your cup of tea, but if you fall back on the principles of voice technique, they will help you get through the experience. After all, what you sound like is not as important as the fact that you will be respecting their business/social customs when you get up and try. You don't have to sound like Frank Sinatra when you sing "My Way," just apply what you know about good voice technique and sing it *your way*. You may even discover that you enjoy it.

Voice Power for the Rising Executive

It is only logical that you will eventually want to move up the ladder, perhaps to a managerial position, and the right voice skills can help in your climb to the top. A good manager must be in control at all times, using a voice that commands respect and projects authority, but one with enough warmth and steadiness to defuse a difficult situation, calm the emotions of others, and convey dissatisfaction without reflecting anger. If you keep yourself centered and your voice supported at all times, emotions will never gain the upper hand. Use the same tone of respect when you talk to subordinates as you would to your superiors in the workplace. Show concern and sympathy without appearing to be condescending.

In addition to cultivating a voice that commands respect, some people find that a voice with some special distinguishing quality can be a tremendous asset. My stepfather came to this country as a young man of eighteen, served in the Army, and lived in Pennsylvania for sixty years, never losing his thick Danish accent. When I asked him why, he claimed it was his strongest calling card in business. No one ever forgot him.

If there is something distinctive about *your* voice, a trait that is uniquely yours or a regional mannerism, develop it into the thumbprint of your signature sound. Use your tape recorder and the advice of friends to help you judge whether this trait is truly an asset and not a liability, as it was to the young computer whiz with the harsh Brooklyn accent.

A Great Motivator

There are going to be times when you want people to do something they are not naturally inclined to do. It could be a request to an employee to put in extra hours on a special project or a pep talk to the sales force encouraging them to meet the sales quota on a new product. The ability to motivate others is one of the skills that must be developed by anyone who wants to advance in an organization. It separates those who are destined for advancement from those who are not.

A great motivator speaks in a way that focuses the mind, stirs the heart, and inspires committed action. To motivate others, you must first be motivated yourself, or at least, *sound* that way. It's about communicating the energy you feel and turning it into action. Those whom you hope to motivate must hear your enthusiasm reflected in the pitch and the pace of your words.

The art of gentle persuasion is more effective than bullying, just as humor and encouragement are more important than anger and threats. Turning negatives into positives is one of the secrets to moving and motivating people. And we must hear this in the tone of your voice. A rising pitch and a lift at the end indicate mounting energy and enthusiasm that will inspire your team to excellence.

Ageism on the Job

"Will you still need me, will you still feed me,
When I'm sixty-four?"

—John Lennon and Paul McCartney
"When I'm Sixty-Four"

What about ageism in the workplace? Currently, we can expect to live to an age that would have seemed ancient one hundred years ago. The average life expectancy for Americans in the year 1900 was forty-seven years. By 1999, it had leapt to an astonishing average of seventy-six years. Improvements in health, nutrition, and medicine have created a generation that is eager and able to remain active in the workplace longer.

Although ageism is against the law, there is little doubt its practice is widespread. In our rapidly evolving economy, we can no longer count on lifelong job security and the most dispensable workers are the first to go. In defense of employers, perhaps ageism doesn't always stem from a conscious decision to discriminate, but rather from an unconscious response to the perception of weakness and loss of vitality. Opportunities come to those who are perceived to be vital and vigorous.

There are three things that signal advancing age and loss of power: posture, gait, and the sound of our voice. They send messages that contribute to an overall impression about our ability to perform. That impression may have little to do with the *reality* of job performance, but much to do with the *perception* of job performance. We can't stop having birthdays, but we can influence the way others perceive us at this stage of our work life by keeping our vital signs strong.

Carry yourself erect; it's never too late to work on your posture. Put a spring in your step and a smile on your face. Be flexible. Change is inevitable, and you must be prepared to accept new ways of doing things. Your speaking skills are certainly something you can control as your age advances. Use the techniques of support and resonance to project a voice that is strong, confident, and full of resonance. There is no reason to speak with a voice that is weak and scratchy when you have the ability to make it hum along smoothly. Don't regard this as trying to appear younger, think instead that you are doing all you can to make it clear that you are a vital and indispensable asset.

Giving Back

Many people experience serious health problems upon retirement. After years of contributing to a job, an alarming number of new retirees seem to languish when life's purpose becomes less clear. Half a millennium ago, artist Leonardo da Vinci remarked, "Life well spent is long." You must continue to give in order to receive satisfaction in life, and the time afforded by retirement is a golden opportunity to give back.

Consider sharing your knowledge with others. You have experience and wisdom that young people won't acquire for another forty years or so. Volunteer your time and services to speak to business and service groups, to counsel young people, and to advise those who need a helping hand. It's a win-win situation—even your voice will benefit. The public nature of these events will require that you keep your voice well exercised and well produced. Others will be richer for it, you'll be richer for it, and chances are you'll live a whole lot longer.

You Are Your Voice

Speaking skills play a role at every stage of a working life. Your voice can empower you or hold you back. You won't be able to conduct your business if no one wants to listen to you or can't understand you. Good vocal management will take you up the ladder, whereas poor vocal skills will leave you stuck on the bottom rung.

Think of this as a *Dress for Success* program for the speaking voice. Your voice makes as much of an impression as your shirt does. If you ignore the power your voice has to further your goals, you might as well show up in your gardening clothes or without combing your hair. But if you make certain that it is dressed for every occasion and sending the right signals, your voice can help you create the image you want to project—one that radiates success appeal.

In Tune With Your World

ONE SUMMER, while I was still a conservatory student, I was asked to sing with a small group at the Monterey Jazz Festival. The unexpected opportunity to perform at this prestigious event fulfilled a long-held dream and I was elated as I drove to the show. Getting to the festival grounds was a breeze; once there, however, I found the parking situation impressively disorganized, even for an outdoor festival. It took half an hour to inch my way to an open spot at the far end of the lot. I didn't mind, though; I was early and it gave me plenty of time to warm up my voice in the car.

I had just parked and locked up when I was approached by a young man asking for the time. Ever polite, and with my mind on other things, I looked down to check my watch when suddenly he grabbed me. My instincts took over and a sound that startled even me commenced. The first time I screamed, he let go of me. The second time I screamed, he dropped my purse and ran off into the night.

At the time, my only concern was for my personal safety. It was much later that I realized how fortunate it was that I had just warmed up my voice, and was supporting well. Not only did the warm-up help me to produce one heck of a bloodcurdling scream, I also hadn't hurt my voice—it was fine when I went onstage a few minutes later to sing.

It is not every day that your trusty voice is required to save property and person from physical harm, but it *is* at the heart of almost every every social encounter. Whether you are exchanging wedding vows, disciplining a determined four-year-old, or about to be robbed in a parking lot, your well-being and happiness may depend on how you sound to others. From morning to night, from birth to the end of our days, our personal lives are filled with situations in which the breathing and speaking skills we've learned will be useful.

Sunrise, Sunset

Why not begin your day by focusing on breathing? When you wake up, take a few minutes to breathe and center yourself—it's a good way to make the transition from the realm of sleep and dreams to that of daily life. Start your day by going over the basics of breathing and voice technique, so that you'll stand a better chance of remembering them during the day. You might also take advantage of this quiet moment to put your day into perspective by reviewing and organizing what you plan to accomplish.

At night, use passive breathing to help you fall asleep more easily. After the lights are out and you've settled into your favorite position, concentrate on breathing effortlessly. Feel the air fall all the way down to your lower abdominal muscles. Any position will do. In fact, lying quietly in the dark could make it easier to find the right muscles.

Very gradually, slow down the pattern of breath by letting the air hover just a bit longer at each end of the inhale/exhale cycle. Don't hold your breath. Just relax and create a space for the air. Contract gently from below to guide it out. As you concentrate on breathing, the steady cadence becomes hypnotic, neutralizing any negative energy left over from your day. Your pulse will slow down, your blood pressure will fall, and before you know it, sheep will be counting *you*.

Special Delivery

During the years that I taught aerobics, several of my co-instructors got married and gave birth to their first children. I devised a breathing program to help them get through pregnancy and delivery with greater ease. Our goals were to (a) retain maximum lower abdominal muscle tone; (b) minimize back strain; (c) improve balance and mobility; and (d) increase the benefits of the delivery room breathing they were learning in Lamaze class.

MUSCLE TONE

We concentrated on passive breathing and low support, constantly flexing and relaxing the lower abdominal muscles. This strengthened those muscles and helped them support the additional weight. These women found that their abdominal muscles remained strong and resilient instead of stretching out and losing elasticity. They were all back teaching aerobics classes within a week or two of delivery and felt they had a complete return to previous muscle tone within a few months.

BACK STRAIN

There is a dramatic shift in body weight during pregnancy that throws the spine out of alignment, resulting in frequent lower back pain. We noticed that tucking under to support reduced a great deal of this unnatural pull of pressure. Those who were diligent about supporting this way were rewarded by a significant reduction in lower back discomfort.

BALANCE

These young women were eager to remain active and mobile throughout their terms of pregnancy, but were justifiably concerned about the possibility of falls. Passive breathing and a low center of gravity seemed to give them a greater sense of balance and more confidence in their mobility.

LAMAZE

"Childbirth is something you do, not something that happens to you," according to Ferdinand Lamaze, the French obstetrician who developed a system for managing the pain of childbirth. Based on relaxation and breath control, the Lamaze method has received widespread acceptance since its conception in the 1950s. All of the young women who taught aerobics with me attended Lamaze classes.

The skills my group had learned seemed to increase the benefits of Lamaze preparation. All that attention to breathing during the months leading up to delivery made it easier for them to concentrate on the fast rhythmic breaths recommended during contractions and to accomplish the deep cleansing breaths that bring oxygen to both mother and baby during delivery.

Once Upon a Time

Bedtime stories present a wonderful opportunity to communicate and bond with a child. A few minutes of private time spent reading to your child at the end of the day will be good for both of you. This is also an excellent time to practice your dramatic speaking skills. Those bedtime stories will come alive when you use color and variety, emphasis, and a wide range of imitative sounds to breathe life into the characters.

But, of course, the primary objective is to put your child to sleep, so use relaxed breathing, your support muscles, and a large measure of resonance to create a warm, mellow tone. Gradually slow down the pace and deliver your story with an increasingly relaxed rhythm that cradles your child to sleep.

Sustained reading, however, can tire your voice quickly unless you use good support to power the sound. To keep from getting hoarse, remember to breathe low and use your lower abdominal muscles. Don't speak from your throat. And make sure you have a glass of water handy to keep your voice well lubricated.

You may choose to send your child off to a peaceful sleep with a lullaby. Use what you know about creating a warm tone to put the "lull" in your lullaby. You don't have to give a big performance, you don't have to know all the words, you don't even have to *use* words—it's the quiet comfort of your voice that matters most to a child.

Speech Is Learned Behavior

I'm often asked why some people speak effortlessly without any training and others seem to have problems all their lives. Although there is probably no single factor that is the cause, there is one idea that interests me. When we first start to find our voice as infants, we tend to imitate those around us. Some people get lucky and learn to speak by imitating a voice that matches their own voice-producing apparatus. Some are not so lucky and imitate a tone that is incompatible with their particular physical structure. Voice problems are the logical result.

Be conscious of the influence the sound of your voice has on the children in your care. Visualize how your voice is being perceived by their ears and processed by their brains. Is that the voice you want them to learn to reproduce?

You can give your offspring a good start in life by passing along what you have learned about Voice Power in this book. Most children breathe low naturally, because they're not obsessed with holding their stomachs in and puffing out their chests as adults are. Don't let that change as they grow up. Encourage your children to acquire good breathing and voice production skills at an early age and to incorporate those skills into their lives.

The Upper Hand

Have you ever thought about how you sound to your kids when you discipline them? How would you rate your voice as a parent? Do your kids (a) *always* listen to you; (b) *sometimes* listen to you; (c) *ever* listen to you; or (d) *never* listen to you? If you have trouble getting their attention, maybe it is because you are using the wrong tone of voice.

It is the *way* in which you say something that makes a big impact on children. If you allow your voice to rise in a question at the end, it sounds as if you're seeking your child's approval. An order should never sound like a request for agreement or approval. Keep your pitch steady and give finality to your commands. When you become impatient, resist the urge to whine. Emphasizing important words with long consonants—"**SSS-top** it **nnn-ow!**"—will get better results than whining, **"St-ah-ah-ah-p."**

Children have good hysteria meters; they're quick to sense when you are out of control. You must learn to disguise your frustration by using breathing and support techniques to create an authoritative tone. And remember, if you make everything sound like a crisis, they're likely to ignore you when it really is important.

Should you find yourself drawn into an intense argument, instead of escalating in volume, you can change the direction of the confrontation by suddenly shifting gears and speaking in a quiet voice. An argument is a consensual duet—it takes two parties to keep an argument alive. If one of you lowers your voice, the whole dynamic changes.

When you're disciplining children, it's a good idea to say what you mean and then stop. They have short attention spans and will tune you out if you ramble on and on. There is a great difference between commanding, "STOP IT *NOW!*" and pleading, "You kids better stop it right now." Be brief and to the point.

To get a child to listen to you, try saying their name in a calm, low, well-supported voice that is followed by a long power pause. That pause will get the child's attention. Then say what you have to say in a low, steady voice, using plenty of consonants to stress the words you want them to heed.

Manners Matter

If you want to pass along a powerful success tool that will give your kids a head start in life, teach them manners. Good manners are a fiendishly clever way to control almost any situation. Anyone who has watched a few cop shows on television has noticed that officers of the law are trained to address people as "sir" or "ma'am" and to use a polite, calming tone at all times. I suppose the assumption is that anyone naïve enough to use good manners couldn't possibly pose a threat.

I live in the South, where a generous dose of "sir" and "ma'am" has been known to smooth over a multitude of difficult situations. Good manners can be deceptively disarming. Anyone who thinks southerners are an easy mark because everyone there sounds so polite is in for a big surprise. It's the ultimate form of control.

Braces and Lisps

Prominent television personality Barbara Walters became renowned for her on-camera interview skills, despite a minor lisp that has plagued her all her life. At one point, she worked to correct it with the help of a speech therapist, but the lisp persisted and eventually became a highly identifiable personal signature. Perhaps her struggle to bring this anomaly under control is reflected in her wonderful command of the spoken word and the thoughtful way she asks questions of those she interviews.

A lisp describes the condition some people experience when they have difficulty pronouncing sibilant letters, especially **S** and **Z**, which soften into a **TH** sound. The problem may be genetic, the result of injury or illness, or the by-product of wearing braces. Braces change the geography of the mouth and suddenly everything feels different. Word articulation may become a challenge.

No matter the source of the lisp, when I'm asked for suggestions to neutralize it, I get good results by asking my students to do the following exercise: Relax the front of your tongue. Now flatten your tongue and extend the sides toward contact with the bicuspids (the fourth teeth back). Pronounce sibilant sounds there rather than at the front of the mouth. The lisp becomes more difficult to detect and often disappears completely.

Metamorphosis

As a child goes through the teenage years, hormonal changes bring about vocal changes. Testosterone causes the larynx to enlarge before the vocal cords have time to catch up with the larger voice box that now holds them. One of the first signs is an unpredictable squeaking or cracking sound.

This change is generally more dramatic in boys than in girls and normally takes place over a year or more, but it may happen quickly with little or no warning. I still remember the time I received a panicked telephone call from the boy soprano I had hired to sing the solos of Leonard Bernstein's *Chichester Psalms* in a concert I was conducting the following day. I heard this low and unfamiliar voice start off with, "Miss Grant-Williams, something happened to me last night. . . ."

The unpredictability of all this squeaking and changing can be embarrassing and disconcerting to a young person. I've found that good support and low breathing seem to make it easier to control this new, lower voice. My advice? Use more power from the lower body, stay out of the throat, and, above all, be patient.

The Dos and Don'ts of Saying "I Do"

Three letters . . . two little words . . . one terrifying moment—saying "I do."

Public speaking isn't easy under normal circumstances, but on the most important day of a young couple's life, it can be utterly intimidating. You are in the spotlight at your wedding ceremony, the central character in what is often a very public performance. You've spent months working on the arrangements. Now, don't you think it might be a good idea to put some thought into how your voice is going to sound when you recite your vows?

Nerves and emotion may conspire to make your voice sound

shaky or feeble, which distracts from what you are saying. But remembering a few simple concepts can guarantee that your wedding vows will ring loud and clear—and even Aunt Mildred in the back will hear them.

There will be much to talk about leading up to the big day. Combine that with an increase in anxiety and you have the makings of a frayed voice. Get plenty of sleep and limit your conversation so that your voice doesn't wear out before the ceremony begins.

Make sure your tears are tears of joy—and not brought on by allergies. If you aren't careful about your choice of flowers, you may find yourself red-eyed and sneezing at the altar. Also, with added stress in the days before your wedding, your immune system may become overwhelmed and more susceptible to colds and sinus problems. Keep sinus and allergy medicine on hand, along with a supply of cough drops and throat lozenges. The last thing you need on that day is a hacking cough and a runny nose—you don't want to sound like a frog when saying "I do" to your prince (or princess).

Remember to breathe! Low relaxed breathing helps you to stay calm. Shallow breathing puts tension around your throat, making it difficult to speak freely. You will sound more convincing when you say your vows if you use energy from your whole body, not only your mouth and throat. In the days before your wedding, practice the breathing and support techniques whenever you speak so that they feel natural when the big day arrives.

On the morning of the ceremony, exercise might be the furthest thing from your mind, but ten minutes set aside for a good stretch and a few basic exercises should get you pumped up and glowing. It will show in the way you carry yourself. And it's a great way to cut down on pre-wedding tension.

The day of your wedding is not the day to starve off those last few pounds—you're going to need your strength—so eat something light a few hours ahead of time. Drink lots of water before the ceremony because the combination of nerves and emotion may give you dry mouth. Keep bottled water handy for a few quick sips before you walk down the aisle.

Pace your words, don't rush what you say. This is your moment, so savor it. Stress the consonants and put plenty of open space around the key words of your vows so they have time to sink in. Most important, don't become so caught up in the moment that you forget *what* you are saying. After all, you've chosen these words to represent one of the most important commitments you will ever make in life. Concentrate on what these words truly mean to you, and that message will carry to everyone present.

I Didn't Catch What You Said

Words are fleeting and temporal, they must be "caught" midair before they can be digested—not an easy feat for everyone. Close to 30 million Americans suffer from hearing loss, yet only one in five owns a hearing aid. And many of those who own one let discomfort and embarrassment deter them from using the devices regularly, if at all. With our graying population and ear-damaging, noise-polluted environment, we can expect to encounter increasing numbers of friends and family who simply do not hear us well.

In the most common form of hearing reduction, the ability to perceive the higher pitches is likely to be impaired, and consonants are especially difficult to discern. When you're speaking to those who are hearing-challenged, use a strong, low-pitched, well-supported voice. Speak clearly and plainly. Lengthen the consonants, especially the aspirated ones—**S, T, F, SH, TH,** and **H.** Allow plenty of room for key words to sink in, and pause to indicate new thoughts or a change in direction. Slow down. If you allow those with hearing loss adequate time to catch what you are saying, your consideration will save you both the frustration of repeating the same conversation over and over again.

Ageless Voice Power

Perhaps "you are as young as you sound" should get equal billing with "you are as young as you feel." Aging doesn't necessarily mean we must croak through the last thirty years of our lives. It's generally not the voice that wears out, but the power behind it that diminishes. If we use good support when we speak and exercise the voice-producing mechanisms regularly to prevent them from atrophying, we will be rewarded with a vibrant and resonant voice well into our later years.

Good breathing techniques are especially important for maintaining balance and grace late in life. As we age, the low sense of gravity that passive breathing gives us can improve our ability to maneuver through daily life injury-free. Better balance through lower abdominal breathing could mean fewer falls, resulting in fewer broken bones.

"I Always Wished I Could Sing . . . !"

If only I had a cheeseburger for every time someone said that to me. I'm going to let you in on a little secret. You can sing if you want to. You don't need a record deal to take pleasure in making music with your voice. You just have to do it. Piano wizard Keith Jarrett put it this way in a 1995 *Time* interview, "Music should be thought of as the desire for an ecstatic relationship to life." Should the idea of an ecstatic relationship to life interest you, go ahead and use the Voice Power techniques to sing if you feel like it. Make the goal pleasure—not perfection.

There was one student who came to me for lessons for more than ten years. Jody Faison had become Nashville's premier restaurateur, at one point owning seven highly successful restaurants. I can't begin to imagine the pressure he was under. When we started, he made it clear that his goal was to do something for himself that would be satisfying and rewarding—he hoped to get a little better at singing. Would he ever sing in public? Maybe. Maybe not. That wasn't the point.

Every week, he would show up for his lesson and forget about everything else for an hour. He didn't have to worry about customers, cooks, or the clean-up crew. He didn't have to wonder whether the wait staff would turn up. He didn't have to yell at anybody. It became a form of therapy for him. For one hour each week, he could concentrate on that ecstatic relationship to life—and go back to his business renewed by it.

Make a Joyful Noise

Whatever your goals, if you're looking for a relaxing and rewarding outlet, try singing. If you've never sung before, these techniques will get you started. If you already sing in church or your community, you'll sing even better. If you've always wanted to reach all the notes in "The Star-Spangled Banner," you might surprise yourself and conquer them at last.

Even someone with a fair to middling singing voice can make a joyful noise at Christmas. The holiday season is the one time of the year when everybody feels most like singing. Relax, have fun. So what if your pitch is off? And who can remember all the words to "O Little Town of Bethlehem" anyway? The point with holiday carols is to celebrate the season with family and friends.

If you're going to be caroling outdoors and it's cold, wear appropriate clothing. Don't get too hot, then cold. Layer your clothing so you can remove some of it or add layers when you go outside. Take a scarf to keep your throat warm and a thermos of warm beverage to help soothe your voice.

Whatever you're singing, think about what the words really mean. It always amazes me how simply thinking about the words can improve the tone. (To learn more about singing, go to www. myvoicecoach.com.)

Best Friends

My love affair with animals started with tadpoles. Convinced they were mermaids, I kept countless numbers of the poor things in mason jars on my nightstand while I breathlessly waited for them to grow long hair and green tails—at age four I believed everything my big sister, Judie, told me. Fortunately, by the time I started dragging home larger pets—puppies from the neighbor's litter and the pastel-colored baby chicks I could never resist at Easter—I had abandoned mason jars and learned a few things about animal care.

In later years, my doorstep became known as the place where people knew they could deposit foundling kittens, injured birds, and lost dogs. I've shared my home with a squirrel monkey, a Muscovy duck named Granny, a Peking nightingale, an exotic Egyptian Mau cat, a succession of stray cats, and quite a few fish. One of the Saluki dogs I bred won top honors for the breed two consecutive years at the prestigious Westminster Dog Show.

Anyone who has lived with pets can easily believe they have a rich emotional life. Animals send and receive complex signals and, just like humans, they love to be talked to. It doesn't matter what you say, as long as you talk to them. What does matter, though, is the tone of your voice. Your voice can soothe, encourage, or depress your pet. The mere tone of your voice can ruin your pet's entire day—or, at least, the next five minutes.

What Your Pet Wants to Hear

Always speak in low, reassuring tones when you approach an animal so it has a sense of your intentions. Your voice tells an animal what to expect from you. It is surprising how oblivious some people are to their effect on animals. They charge right into the animal's space without signaling that their intentions are harmless. Think how large and unpredictable we must appear to the average household pet. If you were swimming next to a blue whale, you would probably be more comfortable if you had a few clues about what it had in mind.

The tone of your voice needs to reflect the response you want from your pet. When playing and cuddling, use soft soothing tones. However, this tone of voice is useless when you need to command or discipline. Do not make your command sound like a question or plea by lifting your voice at the end—you are not politely asking your pet to do something, you are commanding it. As with children, your pet takes its cue from the tone of your voice.

Dogs, especially, are pack animals, and each pack must have a leader. *You* are that leader and must earn the respect of your dog. If you give an urgent command and expect your dog to take heed, that command must sound like a growl. Think about a dog's growl, the sound comes from way down inside, which makes it sound so intimidating. To be convincing, the voice you use must be deep, firm, and sharp. Be sure to take your breath low and use good support so your dog will hear the commitment behind your voice. A training command should also be deep and firm, but without the growl. Don't forget to follow up with a lighter, higher tone as a reward— "Good boy!"

A to Z

This chapter could go on endlessly—covering everything from talking to aliens to talking to zebras—yet still be relevant. Try to imagine getting through life's difficult moments *without* your voice.

You have some useful tools now, so start using them everywhere. If you want them to work, and if you want them to become automatic and feel natural, you must integrate them into everything you do. Begin and end your day with the StressBuster exercise. Take advantage of what you've learned to add another dimension to your self-awareness. It just might make life a little easier and a lot more fun.

voice care

Rx for a
Healthy Voice

I USED to travel as a voice coach with Grammy Award-winning country singer Larry Gatlin, back when he and the Gatlin Brothers were touring heavily. Larry had pushed himself rather hard for years and it was starting to show in his voice. To his credit, he was quite open and public about the problems he was experiencing. Larry and I spent a couple of concentrated weeks working together while he headlined at Harrah's in Reno. Our objectives were to halt the damage and to prevent it from happening again.

We would have a voice lesson each afternoon and later that night I'd run him through his warm-up for the show. I always watched from the wings backstage and took notes on what we needed to cover the next day. We got a lot accomplished that way. But it meant examining long-standing habits and that was hard on him. He would say, "Oh, Renee, when I was twenty-one my voice would just soar out. Everything was so free and easy. I could sing all day and my throat never got tired." I'm sure it was frustrating because the man, indeed, has been blessed with a truly glorious natural voice.

Finally, I said to him: "Gatlin, I see you working out in the hotel gym. I see you at the aerobic workouts I lead for the band. I see the care you put into choosing healthy foods. You work hard to maintain your body as the years go by. What makes you think your voice is any different? It's one more working body part that's affected by everything you do to it and put into it."

Suddenly it made sense to him. He had a fitness regime for his body, now he needed one for his voice, too.

What's the Problem?

Your voice is a living instrument with no readily replaceable parts. It responds to whatever you do to the rest of your body. No rest, and you fatigue it. Not enough water, and your voice can dry out like a thirsty plant. If you strain it, you weaken it. And if you strain it over time, your voice may give out on you altogether. On top of all that, it is subject to constant stress and irritation from both natural and man-made environments over which we have little or no control.

So, how do you ensure that your voice stays healthy and user-friendly? Live by these commonsense basics: Get adequate rest. Make sure your body has plenty of moisture. Eat sensibly. Keep body, brain, *and* voice well exercised.

ZZZZ

Rest. Get it. As much as you can and whenever you can. It's a busy world. We're surrounded by technology that is supposed to make things easier for us, but I don't know anybody who seems to have more free time now than they did ten years ago. And that is the first thing we chip into—our sleep and rest time.

Lack of sleep makes it hard to even think about how we sound. It's not our sole concern when we're struggling to stay awake. Exhaustion affects our posture and body strength. We forget about using energy from our bodies and start speaking using muscles from only the neck up. And when your body is sleep-deprived, it doesn't have the recovery time it needs to resist colds and other respiratory ailments.

Rest, on the other hand, revives your mind and body, recovers energy, replenishes your vital cells, and helps you to relax. For me, the four **R**s of a good night's rest are to *revive, recover, replenish,* and *relax.*

You are the only person who knows how much sleep you need. The standard is eight hours, but ask yourself the following question: If the alarm clock didn't wake you, how long would you sleep? Get the sleep your body tells you that you need to function at your best. In addition to a good night's sleep, don't forget about the rest we get from other sources: naps, work breaks, recreation, and entertainment. Actress and comedian Lily Tomlin once advised, "For fast-acting relief, try slowing down."

Just Add Water

Our bodies, which house our voice mechanisms, are composed of nearly 60 percent water. Therefore, it is vital that we maintain an adequate fluid intake, both internally and externally. Think about caring for your voice the same way you would care for a houseplant. Actually, your voice is somewhat like a plant. If you don't water it, what happens? It croaks.

I love plants, but we didn't get off to a good start together. My sister gave me my first plant when I went off to college. It was good for a laugh. "Meet my roommate, Rhoda . . . Rhoda Dendron." I didn't get to keep it long, though, because the dorm mother claimed it was a pet. It *was* rather large, actually more like a tree than a plant, but, hey, it's not like its bark was keeping the whole dorm awake at night. . . .

Anyway, she ordered me to get rid of it, so I kept it over at a frat house—because when you think "responsible caregiver," you automatically think of frat boys, right? How did it look after a couple of weeks? Some voices remind me of that plant.

The tissues of your throat and mucous membranes must maintain adequate moisture to stay resilient and flexible. Watering your voice is crucial for keeping the cells plumped up and flushing out waste impurities—the process that makes your immune system strong and functional. Dehydration stresses your entire vocal system. Ever feel like you've been gargling with melba toast? What's the solution? Just add water.

Eight Glasses a Day

Human tissue requires a minimum of two and a half quarts of water each day. We get some of that from the food we eat. For example, an egg is roughly 74 percent water, lean meat around 70 percent, and a kernel of wheat, about 6 to 8 percent. Clearly, we can't count on getting all the water we need from food, so we must supplement it by drinking plenty of water.

Drink more water than you think you actually need. Try to drink at least eight glasses a day. If you find that drinking bottled water instead of tap water encourages you to drink more, carry bottled water with you everywhere and actually drink it. Double up on water intake when you are engaged in physical exercise. Compensate for medications that dehydrate. And if you are suffering from a cold or fever, take in extra fluids so that your immune system can work properly.

Let It Rain

Drinking water replaces the fluids in your body internally. Externally, you can create a moisture-rich environment that helps to replace water lost to artificial heat and air-conditioning and the moisture that is absorbed by the walls, carpeting, and furniture of our largely indoor environment. You may notice how much drier your throat feels during the winter. I suggest using a humidifier—they work miracles.

Moisture from a humidifier soothes and relieves sinus and respiratory discomfort. It keeps your throat moist while you sleep. It is good for your skin, nails, and hair as well, so you actually *look* better, too. I recommend using one in the bedroom and perhaps a few others in the rest of your living space. During the winter, my humidifiers pump about sixty gallons of water a week into the air in my Nashville studio. Every year, when spring comes around, I have this fantasy that I'm going to open a closet door one day and find a wall of water waiting to crash down on me. Just where do those sixty gallons a week go?

If you do use a humidifier, it is absolutely crucial that you keep the water fresh. Be sure to clean and disinfect it once a week. Don't let it stand around half full of water and unused for days. Stagnant water is a breeding ground for exotic microbes. You don't want your humidifier pumping those into the air.

Your Piece of the Rain Forest

Another way to increase the moisture level around you is to create your own rain forest. Plants are an excellent way to add moisture to your environment. Think how good you feel outdoors, surrounded by plants and trees. Not many of us live in a rain forest, but we can create our own by bringing plant life into our surroundings, both at home and at work. And, no, plants are not pets—you shouldn't need to walk your ficus tree.

We Are What We Eat

Avoid foods and beverages that dehydrate you. If caffeine and alcohol seem to dry you out, limit your intake. I'm not talking only about coffee. Caffeine comes in many devious forms, so watch out for chocolate, iced tea, soft drinks, and diet pills. But I'm an all-things-in-moderation kind of person. If you love coffee, a cup or two early in the day probably won't hurt you, but three cups of coffee immediately before a big presentation will dry you out—and give you the jitters. Alcohol is also dehydrating, so skip that glass of wine until later in the day.

In addition, alcohol in your system can trigger unpredictable fluctuations in energy levels, making it impossible to support your voice with consistency. If you sense you have a drop in energy after consuming sugar, plan accordingly. A chocolate bar should be your last choice when the pressure is on and you need to count on your voice. Avoid excessively greasy foods and hard-to-digest red protein, which may make you feel bloated and sluggish. Did you know that animal protein takes up to twelve hours to digest? That's a lot of energy your body could be putting toward other things.

Dairy products may cause a different kind of problem because they tend to be mucus-producing. Many singers, including k.d. lang, won't touch dairy products. They say that it "muddies up" their tone. In my experience, some people seem to be mildly allergic to dairy products but may not suffer sufficiently to realize they are being affected. You could be one of them. The next time you drink a glass of milk or have a cup of yogurt, pay attention to how you feel and sound afterward. Experiment when it doesn't matter so that you are prepared when it does.

Food allergies can turn up anywhere. Many people experience an adverse reaction to monosodium glutamate (MSG) and other food additives. Be wary of products that contain yeast, whey, soy, and enzymes. If I don't want to start wheezing when I go out to eat, I must tell the wait staff in advance that "I'll stop breathing" if they serve me something with MSG in it. Sometimes, it actually works. But since my special order means that the kitchen would need to start from scratch with fresh ingredients, they usually sneak it in somewhere and I end up wheezing anyway.

Eat a good balance of protein and carbohydrates. Salads, fruits and vegetables, light protein—chicken or fish—and carbohydrates in moderation are best. They make you feel light instead of heavy. It's no surprise that these are the foods recommended to make you lighter and thinner on a weight-loss program. Pay attention to your body and find out what affects you.

What Is GERD?

You may be surprised to learn that chronic Gastroesophageal Reflux Disease (GERD) is sweeping the country in epidemic proportions. In this condition, the stomach's digestive acids back up and rise too high in the throat and air passages. They literally burn the sensitive membranes of the throat and esophagus.

Depending on the source, current estimates indicate that anywhere from 30 percent to a whopping 49 percent of us suffer from the effects of reflux. Many people may not realize that they are suffering from this condition because GERD is often confused with other disorders. It might register first as simple, temporary heartburn—easy to ignore. But if you find yourself reaching for the antacids more than once a week, this could be a sign of a more serious problem.

There is growing interest in the damage that can happen to the voice from this often-ignored disorder. Untreated, it may cause hoarseness, sore throat, laryngitis, and chronic cough. When it gets into the respiratory system, its symptoms resemble those of bronchitis and asthma. And indeed, severe reflux may actually develop into chronic bronchitis or asthma. It is now also considered a leading culprit in the occurrence of throat and lung cancer.

Like heartburn, this condition is directly related to our eating habits. Acidic foods like citrus fruits and tomato products, fatty foods, alcohol, caffeine, chocolate, overeating, and eating late at night contribute to excessive acid reflux. Spicy foods are especially corrosive. *(Could the rise in incidence have something to do with the fact that salsa sauce now outsells ketchup as America's leading condiment?)* If you think that you may be at risk, change your habits and avoid these foods. Above all, consult your doctor. There are new methods of diagnosis available and acid reflux can be treated in a number of ways before it has a chance to permanently damage your voice.

In short, everything that you put into your body affects you. Put a higher grade of gasoline into your car and your engine will run smoother. Put a healthier diet into your body and your voice will respond accordingly. Sputtering and choking are not what we want to hear in a car *or* in a voice.

Use It or Lose It

Regular exercise does more than build strength and muscle mass. It boosts your metabolism. It increases your sense of well-being and makes you feel stronger about using energy from your body when you speak. And it is a wonderful way to cut down on tension.

If you already engage in a regular exercise program, I applaud you. Regular exercise not only helps you to live longer but also helps you to live longer *better*. Comedian George Burns exercised every day, usually by swimming laps wherever he was. It kept a twinkle in his eye for nearly a century. Musician Bob Weir improvised with whatever was available to keep in shape when the Grateful Dead was touring. When we worked together, we would utilize the stairs of the hotel for exercise—run up the stairwell and take the elevator down. Over and over. Next time you travel, try it—but only after checking with your doctor, of course.

If you're pressed for time, you can get a decent workout in your own home. Stair-stepping machines, weights, treadmills, or other basic exercise equipment will help to keep you in shape—*if* you use them. Try for a good balance of stretching, aerobics, and strength building. Any legitimate program will work if you stick with it. On a day when you know you're going to demand a great deal from your voice, make time for a good stretch to keep you limber and a light workout that will get you pumped up, ready for the physical demands of the day.

Victims of Vocal Abuse

Even a healthy voice will rebel if you strain it. Tired vocal cords become irritated and swollen. Continue the abuse and they lose their elasticity. They may refuse to press together as they should to make a clean sound. If you often find yourself hoarse at the end of a long day or constantly feel the urge to clear your throat—or are about to undergo surgery on your vocal cords—it is possible that you are a victim of vocal abuse. What can you do?

When your surroundings are noisy, limit what you say. Don't

risk damaging your voice by pushing it too hard, especially in bad acoustic situations. In the car, don't try to talk over the radio *and* the kids. At a noisy party or concert, enjoy the music and forget about carrying on a high-decibel conversation.

It is tempting to yell in some situations. But like all temptations, there is usually a price to pay—it tears up your throat. Don't get carried away at sports events. My friend Jonell is a big sports fan and often screams and yells so much at football games that she can't talk the next day.

Sometimes yelling is a big part of anger. When you lose your temper, don't yell at the kids, the dog, the cat, or your spouse. It's hard on your voice and, besides, it doesn't work very well. Try to say as little as possible when you're upset. Intense emotions make you lose control and the less you say, the better off you'll be all the way around. You can save your voice and maybe a friendship, too.

Don't overdo it when you're under the influence of alcohol. Two glasses of wine can loosen your tongue, making you unaware of how much you're talking and how loud you've become. May I suggest a good rule of thumb? Never start a sentence with, "You know what your problem is?"

When you're on the telephone, try not to shout. Some people seem to forget they're using the telephone and think that they need to shout to be heard in Des Moines. As well as straining your voice, it can be painfully annoying to the person on the other end of the line. Of course, that might keep the conversation short. Surprisingly, although shouting is bad for your voice, my doctor says that whispering is the worst thing you can do. Pressure from prolonged whispering irritates and inflames the vocal cords.

Avoid resting the telephone between your head and shoulder. Sure, it frees up your hands for getting things done while you talk, but it throws your neck off-balance and strains muscles that affect your voice. Try using a portable headset instead.

Silence is the ultimate in saving your voice. You *do* have the right to remain silent.

Just What Are Nodes?

Voice abuse can lead to a condition called *nodes*, which is a serious problem that often plagues singers. Throat nodes form like calluses. They're a protective layer of compacted, dead skin cells, caused by repeated friction and pressure—something like the calluses you would get on your hands if you worked too long in the garden. Let's say you work with a shovel; after a while, your hands build up a layer of calluses to protect themselves from the friction. As long as you keep shoveling, calluses keep building. They don't begin to fade until you stop. Vocal cords develop calluses, too.

When strain or friction irritates your throat, the first thing your body does is send down a bit of mucous to lubricate it. That's why people feel the need to clear their throats after yelling. It's as if the body is saying, "Okay, I hurt, so let's try a protective salve here." If you keep abusing your voice and clearing your throat, the body then says, "Okay, I guess that's not working. Let's build a callus to protect this area." The problem now is that the callus gets in the way and prevents your vocal cords from fitting together cleanly—your voice begins to sound hoarse and unpredictable. You've developed a node.

Clearing your throat can actually contribute to nodes because it puts a double burden on your vocal cords. First, it wipes away your throat's initial defense mechanism, the lubricating fluid your body responds with. And then, the pressure you apply to your cords to clear them actually irritates and causes them to swell. If you feel you must clear, please be gentle.

Like calluses, nodes will shrink and go away, but complete vocal rest over an extended period of time is required. Some people choose instead to have them surgically removed. However, if you don't correct the source of the problem—the abuse that put them there in the first place—they'll simply re-form. Then you have to deal with scar tissue from the surgery as well.

Let me tell you about Kim Wilson, lead singer of the Fabulous Thunderbirds. You may be familiar with the group's hit song, "Tuff Enuff." Kim is an energetic blues/rock singer. Singing from his throat for years had damaged his voice and he decided to have surgery to remove the nodes that had formed. The surgery cleared up his problem for a while. But because he didn't dramatically change the way he sang, he developed the same condition again a couple of years later. Only now, scar tissue from the surgery compounded the problem. Kim was at the height of his career and not anxious to have another surgery, only to be faced with the same situation again in two more years. He started wondering whether he should think about a new profession.

Austin singer Toni Price told him about my work. After a brief meeting, we decided that he should come to Nashville, where we began an intensive two-week program. He even stayed in my guest room. A month later, he came back and we did the same routine. Then I went out to Sky Walker Ranch Studio near San Francisco and worked with him while he was cutting the vocals for a new album he was recording at the time. Kim was very serious and worked hard to use more of his body to sing. We got him back on track and he no longer needed to undergo surgery.

Singers often get to this point in their careers: They sound great and are making great records. Then their lives change drastically. Other demands intrude. They begin to tour heavily. They have a public to cultivate. They're already singing well enough to be on a record label so they think, "Okay, the voice is fine, I'll worry about these other things now instead." Although it is understandable, it is still a bad decision. Life on the road, in addition to the demands of a successful career, can be difficult to handle. Too many singers lose the healthy voice that got them there in the first place.

First Aid for Sore Throats

Resist using anesthetizing lozenges or sprays to numb a sore throat. A sore throat is nature's way of saying, "Pay attention. Something is wrong." We've all heard about athletes who have been shot so full of anesthetics that they couldn't feel the pain and consequently reinjured themselves. Without pain to alert you, you may be tempted to overuse your voice, causing serious damage to an area that originally might have been only mildly irritated.

Chew gum or a piece of hard candy to get the juices flowing. Or try a nonanesthetizing throat spray or lozenge. Gargling with warm salt water will bring down the swelling in your throat. Don't make it overly hot, but hot enough to work. The best thing for a sore throat is to keep your mouth closed. Don't talk, don't speak, don't sing, don't weep, don't sneeze, don't whisper, and don't clear your throat. Just keep your mouth shut and give your voice a chance to recover. If you feel the need to communicate, use this time to catch up on your e-mail or actually write a letter.

Cold Season

My mother was good at getting us to bundle up when we went out to play. Every year on the first nice spring day she terrorized us with the same story about some poor child she claims to have known:

> "And she went out without her scarf and her coat was wide open and she caught a cold and then she got pneumonia and DIED!"

Every spring, we could always count on the daffodils and that story. Pretty much word for word. In fact, the story was more reliable than the daffodils. But it worked on us kids. And that is the subject I want to discuss now—colds.

During cold season, viruses are practically endemic. They're "in the air" wherever we interact with other people. It is impossible to avoid them—unless we happen to be a wealthy recluse like Howard Hughes. They attack us. Our body's defense mechanisms fight them off. When our resistance is compromised, we become vulnerable. It never hurts to have a few tricks up your sleeve when nasty weather and even nastier viruses team up against you. We have two main lines of defense: (a) maximizing our resistance; and (b) minimizing our exposure.

For maximum resistance to viruses, go back to the basics of getting adequate rest and drinking plenty of fluids. Eat sensibly. And breathe. Don't forget to open up and breathe. Also, try to maintain a fairly consistent body temperature.

Each person's reaction to abrupt temperature change is different. Rapid changes in body temperature make me susceptible to colds and sinus problems—you may feel that is true for you, too. Don't allow yourself to get too hot, and then chilled. Resting in an air-conditioned room after overheating can be a recipe for disaster. If you are going outdoors and it is cold, wear appropriate clothing. Layering gives you options. You can remove a coat or heavy sweater when you're inside so that you do not overheat. Just add the layers when you go back outside again.

Drafts can be sneaky. I find I'm more susceptible to colds when I'm caught in a draft. Watch out for drafty restaurants where the cold breeze keeps both the wait staff and the customers moving along. It's an old restaurant trick designed to get customers in and out quickly. Considering that digestion further lowers body temperature, it's easy to become chilled. Don't be afraid to ask for another table away from the fan or to have the air-conditioning taken off the sub-zero setting.

Carrier's Curse

In warm weather we face an interesting dilemma. Most air-conditioned buildings are kept much colder than the air outdoors, often to the point of discomfort. If we dress for the heat of the day, we could freeze to death stuck in an air-conditioned building later on.

Willis Carrier, the visionary U.S. inventor who dedicated his business life to developing an air cooling system that would be affordable to everyone, thought he was doing a wonderful thing. And indeed, he was. Air-conditioning has substantially increased our comfort and productivity. It is sometimes difficult to believe that it hasn't been around forever. But like many of our modern improvements on nature, there is a downside. *(Just to warn you, I'm back on my soapbox again.)*

Air-conditioning isolates us from our neighbors. We're locked up inside our temperature-controlled cars and houses. Look at the streets and yards in most suburban areas. Nobody sits on the porch. Children don't play outside. Neighbors don't interact. Air-conditioning separates us from the great outdoors and from each other. Our dependency on air-conditioning has created so-called sick buildings. When we recycle the air in our high-rise buildings, we also risk recycling microbes and pollutants.

Air-conditioning also takes a toll on the ozone layer, which protects us from being fried by harmful rays of the sun. Gazillions of chlorofluorocarbons—the waste by-product of air-conditioning—have contributed to blowing a dangerous hole in the ozone layer that may never be reversed in our lifetime. This means that we and our children will be paying for our current comfort by facing an increased risk of contracting skin cancer and suppressed immune systems in the future. It makes catching a cold seem like a small concern in the face of potential planetary demise.

Comfort is one thing, but ask yourself, how cold does it have to be to be comfortable? And is excessive air-conditioning really worth the added risks? Maybe it doesn't need to be quite so cold indoors. *(Okay, I'm off my soapbox now.)*

Minimize Your Exposure

The second line of defense is to take precautions that minimize your exposure. During cold season, limit your contact with sick people. This can be difficult in our busy world, but you're not doing them any favors if you get sick, too. Shared telephones are fertile breeding grounds for germs. It's a very intimate thing to put your mouth exactly where another person has been speaking. Try practicing "safe speaking" by using disposable hand sanitizers to clean off the mouthpiece before you use someone else's telephone or let them use yours.

Wash your hands thoroughly and wash them often. Hand sanitizers can be a convenient way to disinfect in a pinch. Carry your own pen with you when you go shopping or to the bank. It is impossible to know what type of microbe the last person might have left on the pen at the counter. Also, there are few items of more questionable origin than the paper money that circulates among us. Handle it with care and wash up afterward. You never know where it's been.

Now, I don't want to ruin the party here, but I'm also on a crusade to do away with the tradition of putting candles on a birthday cake. Think about it. "Here, just let me blow on this before I offer you a piece."

Zinc Lozenges

If you do catch a rhinovirus-induced cold, there may be something you can do about it. Back in 1985, I picked up a flier in a health-food store in Carmel, California. It reported a study made by the American Society of Microbiology after an unexpected occurrence.

Zinc, in lozenge form, had been administered to a six-year-old child as part of her treatment for leukemia. The cold she had that morning seemed to vastly improve by nightfall. This led to studies concluding that zinc, taken in lozenge form, proved to be extremely effective at reducing both the severity and the duration of colds, as well as preventing and actually terminating colds.

I was very interested because, at the time, I was on a long sales trip in California. And it had rained at least forty days and forty nights, I swear. I could feel myself starting to get those first scratchy feelings of a cold. I took the zinc and was amazed. It stopped the cold in its tracks. Now I reach for zinc at the first sign of a cold. It works well for me. Once I even went four and a half years without getting a cold.

Zinc destroys the rhinovirus on contact so it does no good if you swallow it in pill form. Let the lozenge dissolve slowly. Resist the urge to chew it up like candy. The zinc must come into contact with the virus in the tissues to work. Even if the cold already has you in its grip, start taking them as soon as you can and it should shorten the duration of the symptoms. The brand I take contains 12.5 milligrams of zinc and I take up to eighteen a day when I'm fighting a cold, or one an hour. Not all brands taste great, so you may need to experiment to find one that is compatible with your taste buds. Or try one of the new zinc nasal sprays.

Other Remedies

And yes, generations of mothers were right after all, chicken soup really does help. It's the amino acid cysteine in chicken soup that helps you to recover. But even if it didn't actually work, you might still get a good placebo effect. What is the placebo effect? Just remember this: Things don't always have to work—to work!

Many people get positive results from natural and homeopathic remedies. You might see whether your immune system receives a boost from herbs like echinacea and goldenseal or from vitamin C. Above all, use common sense. Get lots of rest. Load up on fluids. Turn on your humidifier. You may not feel like eating, but keep your strength up with light nourishing foods.

And don't be one of those people who thinks the company will go out of business if you take a sick day. You're not helping the bottom line if you show up and infect the rest of the office, so pamper yourself for a few days. A respiratory ailment can turn nasty very quickly. Stay in touch with your doctor. And keep away from the people you care about or you'll be taking care of them *next* week.

Influenza

Sometimes it is hard to distinguish influenza from a good old-fashioned cold. Flu symptoms often include a high fever or chills and sweats. Muscles all over your body ache. Everything hurts. Your head, your eyes, and even your scalp can hurt. Doctors refer to the flu as the Mack truck syndrome. As in, "Doctor, I feel like I've been hit by one." If it's a bout of the flu that hit you, all bets may be off. None of the remedies I've mentioned may work with the flu. My advice would probably be the same as your doctor's: lots of rest and liquids. And get a flu shot.

While listening to a researcher from the Centers for Disease Control and Prevention (CDC) one evening, I was shocked to learn how far in advance they must start to prepare the vaccine. Influenza takes many diverse forms every year, and the vaccine can inoculate against only a few strains of the virus. The manufacture and distribution process is time-consuming and must begin long before flu season.

As early as January, final decisions are made about which of the flu strains coming out of Asia *this* year they will inoculate against in the *following* season's vaccine. So, after examining the thirty to forty strains they can identify, they take their best guess about which ones will travel to the United States and cause the most trouble starting the following November. This CDC researcher freely admitted that there is a great deal of hit and miss involved. Sometimes they do well and cover the most virulent strains, sometimes they get only a few, and sometimes they miss by a mile.

Still, your best defense is to get your annual flu shot early and hope you've been vaccinated against the strain that will turn up in your town. It's not foolproof, but it's currently the best protection we have. Check with your doctor to make certain that you're not allergic to other substances that may be found in the vaccine.

If you get the bug anyway, see whether you might be a candidate for some of the new prescription and over-the-counter drugs designed to shorten the influenza cycle. Or try oscillococcinum. It's a homeopathic remedy touted by many for reducing the worst symptoms of the flu.

Allergies

In an average year, what affects 50 to 60 million people, is responsible for 3.5 million lost workdays, and costs more than two billion dollars? If you guessed allergies, you are correct.

Allergies are the sixth leading cause of chronic disease in the United States. We're allergic to mold, dander, plant pollen, cats, smoke, cats who smoke, insect stings, medications, and even certain foods. Allergens are serious business. They attack us in three ways: (a) through the air with pollen, dust, and mold; (b) when insects inject us with venom; and (c) through the ingestion of food and medication.

Allergic reactions might affect our speaking mechanism by producing an inflamed throat, a stuffy head, or by reducing our ability to breathe freely. What can we do to combat allergies and their debilitating effects? Let's look at the different pathways allergens use to enter our bodies and see what we can do to prevent these attacks.

We'll start with pollen, animal dander, dust, and molds. To keep these airborne pests at bay, I recommend purchasing air purifiers for your home and office. Look for the type that has a high-efficiency particulate air (HEPA) filter. Dust your furniture frequently, using a moist rag that lifts the dust and carries it away rather than fluffing it back into the air.

If you have bare floors, use a vacuum and damp mop instead of a broom. Vacuum carpets regularly or, even better, do away with carpet all together and go with hardwood floors. Plastic covers over mattresses and pillows cut down on the number of microscopic mites that live on dander. Keep your bedding clean and see whether you can get Fido to sleep somewhere else.

I don't think I have to go into the other dangers associated with cigarette smoking, but as far as your voice is concerned, cigarette smoke can trigger an allergic reaction that irritates and inflames your vocal cords. Elvis Presley got it right when he said, "A singer'd have to be crazy to [smoke], and I can't think of why anyone else'd want to." So, don't smoke, and avoid secondhand smoke whenever you can.

Even airborne particles from other sources can be dangerous. I didn't realize I was allergic to sawdust until the day I was singing in a rather arty concert at a Northern California gallery. A dancer in the audience spontaneously got up and started doing an interpretive modern dance to our music. The first thing she did was light a big stick of incense and plop it down on the edge of the stage, right under my nose. By the end of the concert, my throat had swollen so much that my voice had dropped about an octave and I was doing quite a good Godzilla imitation. I learned later that incense is made from sawdust.

To determine whether you are susceptible to allergies through ingestion, keep a diary of the foods you eat and their effect on you. If you don't feel up-to-snuff after eating the same type of food several times, you may be allergic. Have your doctor run tests if you suspect your favorite foods bother you. Combating insects is more direct. Cover up and use an insect repellent whenever you're outside. Your doctor or pharmacist should be able to recommend a brand that is safe for you.

It is widely thought that stress and emotional turmoil play a role in allergic reactions, although there are no conclusive studies to support that assumption. There might be some benefit from applying passive breathing relaxation techniques to boost your resistance. It couldn't hurt to try.

And if you have allergies and sinus problems, sorry, but you probably shouldn't move to Nashville, where I live. For reasons geological, Nashville is the sinus and allergy capital of the known universe. Our state flower should be the mold spore and the new statue down at City Hall, a giant box of Kleenex!

Sinus Infections

Sometimes a sore throat indicates a sinus infection. A severe headache in the frontal area is a typical sign of acute sinusitis. When mucus is trapped in the sinus area, it becomes a breeding ground for bacteria, which then can travel downward to affect your throat. The sore throat is not always the problem, but rather may be a symptom. The most common treatment usually involves taking a decongestant in pill form. The drawback is that you're drugging your entire body for something that affects only your nose and throat.

Here is a trick I've discovered that appears to clear up certain sinus infections. It probably won't work if your sinus problems are caused by allergies, but if they're coming from a bona fide rhinovirus infection, it may work for you. We're going to destroy the rhinoviruses where they live in the sinus nasal tissue. Take an 8 1/2- by 11-inch sheet of paper and roll it into an inverse cone, like a megaphone. Use a piece of tape to hold it together. Now plug in your hair dryer and have a seat. Place the hair dryer nozzle in the larger end and use the cone to send warm air directly up your nose. (*Of course, this might make the other people in the hair salon a little nervous, but pay no attention to them.*)

Inhale the heat through your nose for about three minutes. Inhale deeply. Get that area as hot as you can tolerate without burning yourself. Repeat the process several times during the next twenty-four hours. The goal is to heat up the sinus area—much as the entire body heats itself up when it creates a fever as a defense against infectious invasion. Your body creates a fever so that the host environment becomes too hot for the virus to survive.

Haven't you noticed how much better you feel when a fever breaks? That is because your body eventually becomes too hot for the invaders to live and they all croak at once. But be careful not to burn yourself. Regulate the heat the way you would if you were gargling. When you gargle with hot salt water for a sore throat, you need to make it hot enough to do some good, but not so hot that it burns your throat. Use common sense—and don't burn your nose.

This hair dryer "miracle cure" seems to work well on genuine infections of the sinus area, but doesn't work as well on a sinus attack that comes from allergies. Many people suffer from both and it's hard to tell them apart. It's worth a try in case it might be infection-based. Don't give up if it doesn't work on the first attempt. And see a doctor if you feel there is a reason for concern.

Call Me in the Morning

Even with the best precautions, we all get sick sometimes. You would be wise to develop a relationship with a good ear, nose and throat specialist. Many respiratory symptoms are similar, making it difficult to diagnose the flu, allergies, or a cold without the aid of a doctor. A sore throat, persistent cough, or weakened voice could indicate a more serious disorder, such as strep throat, a broken blood vessel, pneumonia, chronic bronchitis, tuberculosis, asthma, emphysema, Lyme disease, or even cancer. These conditions require prompt medical attention. Don't fool around. If you have any reason to believe your problem could be serious, see a doctor. Self-diagnosis is dangerous.

Prescription for a Healthy Voice

We've talked about the dangers of a voice in trouble, but what are the rewards of a healthy voice? Well, your throat doesn't hurt when you speak. You don't have to wait until lunchtime for the cobwebs to clear out. Your voice doesn't give out on you every day around three o'clock. You never get raspy. You seldom have to clear your throat. And you might not get every cold that blows through town.

Begin paying close attention to the things that affect your voice. Then keep track of what works for you. Start your own personal voice journal. Make a record of all the times you have problems with your voice, and what may be contributing to those problems. Does it have anything to do with your diet, your sleep habits, or your environment?

Watch out for situations that encourage you to abuse your voice. Note problems as they occur and factors that are present in your life at the time. Then record what happens when you follow the guidelines you've learned in this chapter. Problems that started because of your speaking habits will simply recur if you don't change the habits that caused them in the first place. Go back to Chapter 2 and Chapter 3 and review the breathing, support, and resonance techniques.

By no means is this chapter intended to be a complete vocal health program—what works for one person might not work for you—but it's a good starting point. Use common sense when it comes to your voice. Remember the basics. Get adequate rest. Get plenty of moisture. Eat sensibly. Keep body and voice well exercised. Remember to breathe. Maintain a constant body temperature. Maximize your resistance while minimizing your exposure. And resist the temptation to yell, even if your kid's Little League coach truly *is* an idiot.

Epilogue

Every voice has a so-called thumbprint, or an identifying sound. And just like the background music that underscores the action in a movie, that sound sets the stage for effective communication. In your personal life, a dynamic speaking voice is an asset. In business, it is crucial. Regardless of your job title, your voice makes an indelible impression on everyone you encounter and is central to the image you project in the business world. Remember, it's not always what you say, but *how* you say it, that counts. Worthy people are often overlooked because their speaking skills represent them poorly.

Think of how much we covered in this book: We examined all the basic building blocks of a great speaking presence, including both tone and delivery. We learned about breathing, and how to use it to center ourselves. We learned to support, resonate, and visualize the sound. We discussed emphasizing individual words through consonants and using silence as a communication tool. We have seen how conflict and resolution add color and variety to whatever we say.

But it all starts with breathing. Breath is the force behind your speaking voice, the steam that drives your engine and the wind that fills your sail. It's the foundation for all the Voice Power techniques we learned. Pay special attention to your breathing, because once you begin breathing correctly, everything else will fall into place.

After you've had an opportunity to assimilate what you learned, revisit the Voice Power quiz in Chapter 1. If I've done my job well, your score should be significantly higher this time. Find your original recording and the list of qualities you heard in your voice. Make another recording. What do you hear now?

I compiled these techniques and guidelines after listening to and observing what works for singers. They can work for you too, but only if you incorporate them into your life and actually use them. Your goal should be the voice nirvana of unconscious competence. Have I taught you how to speak? I don't think of it that way. I think of it as removing barriers that might be holding you back, and preventing you from making the most of your own voice.

Experiment. Listen to others. Start noticing what makes other voices interesting and compelling. Don't be afraid to throw a few curves now and then. Rules are meant to be broken. You have to *imagine* yourself as interesting to *be* interesting. Whatever else she may or may not have been, Miranda—the unattractive social worker who pretended to be a glamorous heiress—probably wasn't a monotone.

Remember, your voice is one third of the impression you make. You know what to do now. Make that one third count.

Index

About the Author

Voice coach Renee Grant-Williams has been the subject of a CBS profile, appeared on network, syndicated, and cable television programs, and hundreds of radio stations. Ms. Grant-Williams, a member of the National Speakers Association, has written for and appeared in numerous national publications.

Her clients include attorneys, public speakers, actors, salespeople, and politicians. Fifteen years of experience as national director of sales for prominent film and music production companies—successfully marketing campaigns to Disney, Kraft, Blockbuster, General Motors, American Airlines, and countless others—has taught her first-hand that positive voice techniques translate into good business.

She has worked with well-known entertainers like the Dixie Chicks, Faith Hill, Tim McGraw, Christina Aguilera, Randy Travis, Huey Lewis, Linda Ronstadt, Charlie Daniels, Martina McBride, Lyle Lovett, Larry Gatlin, and Bob Weir of the Grateful Dead. She has been a consultant to nearly every major record label.

Ms. Grant-Williams is also an accomplished vocalist and musician herself. A graduate of the San Francisco Conservatory of Music, she later taught there as well as at the University of California, Berkeley, where she was the director of the Division of Vocal Music.

Renee Grant-Williams lives in Nashville, Tennessee, and may be contacted at 800-467-0490 or at www.MyVoiceCoach.com.